RECIPES & TIPS FOR

SUSTAINABLE LIVING

with STACY HARRIS

LR
LIVING READY BOOKS
IOLA, WISCONSIN
www.LivingReadyOnline.com

Published by

Living Ready, an imprint of F+W Media, Inc.
700 East State Street • Iola, WI 54990-0001
715-445-2214 • 888-457-2873
www.livingreadyonline.com

Other fine Living Ready books are available from your local bookstore and online suppliers.
Visit our website at www.livingreadyonline.com

ISBN-13: 978-1-4402-3555-9
ISBN-10: 1-4402-3555-4

Cover Design by Dave Hauser
Designed by Sharon Bartsch

Printed in China

Thanks

One of my favorite things to do is to share tried-and-true recipes and tips for the sustainable lifestyle in a way that is fun and beautiful. Thankfully, I am surrounded with the most brilliant, talented, and creative people I have ever known. Working on a cookbook is not an individual endeavor, but quite a collaboration of many creative minds. I would like to thank those creative people who have poured their energy into developing exactly what I have envisioned.

First is my wonderful husband who encourages me in every enterprise I set my heart on accomplishing and for supporting me in every way possible. He is the creative mind that brings all my thoughts together in an amazing way. Second are my children, Hunter, Hampton, Graylyn, Howlett, Mary Elizabeth, Anna Julia, and Milly. They have all played a role in the making of this book from the planting, saving, and harvesting of the seeds and vegetables, to the cooking of the recipes, cleaning the kitchen, and anything and everything asked of them. I could not ask for more in my children. They are my heart and inspiration for all my projects and are the delight of my life.

There's also the fabulous team of publishers and editors that produced the book — David Blansfield, president; Jamie Wilkinson, group publisher whose encouragement I could not have done without; the designers, Dave Hauser and Sharon Bartsch, who created a beautiful book; and my publicist, Meaghan Finnerty. Thank you so much for producing the best book possible, for believing in me, and being excited about this project.

Finally, I would like to thank Alan Clemons, the incredible writer who introduced me to Jamie Wilkinson. I would also like to thank my mom, Paula Johnson, who has supported me through the development of my books and my dad, Wayne Pilgreen, who is the inspiration for much of the book. Lastly, I would like to thank David Robertson for the beautiful photographs of my family. I am blessed and thankful to be surrounded with such talent and inspiration.

Contents

Introduction

As I sit here on the porch writing, I am watching Anna, my six year old, playing with the chickens and turkeys, while several of my other kids are picking salad greens from the garden for tonight's supper. How do I find myself in this blissful life after growing up with career-minded parents preparing me for a life as an attorney and who did not even like to cook, much less garden? My husband, Scott, has always been a "Daniel Boone" of sorts. His life begins and ends with the outdoors, and he is a very self-sufficient type of guy. I, on the other hand, was more of a city girl who happened to fall "head over heels" for this "land and animal loving" outdoorsman. We married during my last semester in law school, and thankfully, my life changed directions forever! Our first of seven children arrived soon after our first anniversary. Never before had I wanted optimal health for myself and my family. We were already eating wild game, but I began to see the necessity for other healthy sustainable foods even more now that we had a baby to care for. I began to enjoy this natural and self-sufficient lifestyle more and more. It is very empowering to know that I could sustain my own life with the knowledge I have gained through the years. I have learned to shoot a gun, till the land, grow the perfect heirloom beefsteak tomato, raise baby chicks, nurture bees, preserve all that I harvest, forage wild mushrooms, and cook the freshest, most succulent dishes known to man...at least my husband. I am continuing to learn to live the self-sustainable life, and it continues to transform my life and fill me with REAL, useful, life-giving information that liberates my soul. The dirt, animals, sun, and rain have become my friends.

Historically, just about every home had a kitchen garden and a few chickens in the back yard, if not out of necessity, merely for the pleasure of raising nutritious food for their families. As our lives have gotten busier and space increasingly sparse, people have relied on supermarkets for their food source. Supermarket produce and meat are subpar to the simply grown vegetables, eggs, and meat of the backyard garden. Besides most of the supermarket

game healthier, their taste is superior to their supermarket counterparts. Fresh, unaltered fruits, vegetables, home grown chickens, eggs, and game meat are truly the only choice for my family. The small effort that you can invest in raising and harvesting your own food far outweighs any sacrifices of time or energy that it may require. Really, it is no sacrifice at all considering the enjoyment of being so closely connected to nature.

Scott and I have taught our children to truly enjoy all kinds of foods, especially those that are perfectly fresh from the garden, woods, or water. They all take part in the entire process of harvesting food for the table, whether it be planning the garden, saving seeds, fishing, or bringing in vegetables and herbs from the garden. When kids take part in their own sustenance, they want the pleasure of enjoying it to the fullest with great recipes. They are competent in the lost art of harvesting and preserving their own foods and are able to make wise choices as to their food sources. Our family's greatest memories are always centered around food. I was blessed to have a grandmother who passed her traditional Southern preparation of food down to me. Many have the blessings of cherishing not only the recipes that have been passed down to them, but also the heirloom seeds that have been saved from year to year from their grandparents' favorite plants. How awesome is that? What a legacy! We have not had to force our children to work with us in planting and harvesting the garden. Quite the opposite. They feel that they are missing out on the fun if they are not with us. I am still, like a

fruits and vegetables being genetically modified and sprayed with pesticides, they have also lost much of their nutritional value and taste once they reach the supermarket shelves. Additionally, most of the supermarket proteins are full of antibiotics and hormones, leaving wild game and fish as my obvious preference of protein. The diet of wild game is perfectly natural and perfect for our bodies, just as God planned it. Not only are naturally harvested crops and

fascinated child, in awe each time that I plant a seed and watch it grow from a seedling to a full-grown plant producing sustenance for my family.

The self-sustainable lifestyle is one that contributes to superior food and health, extraordinary competence, responsibility, and financial stability, as well as gives us a connection with our ancestors, families, and the land. I am a believer that home should be a place of industry, adventure, and rejuvenation to be of better service to others. What better way to fulfill this purpose than to be self-sufficient and share the abundance with those around me? The satisfaction of tilling the ground, planting a seed, watching it grow and produce flavor and health-giving food is one of the most treasured blessings in life that I want to pass down for generations to come. Using God's natural resources that He so bountifully supplies is a privilege and honor that inspires me to be a "keeper" of the land. My hope for you is to start with the basics of at least cooking with fresh vegetables and free-range animals, or for those who are seasoned gardeners to continue on your journey to health and self-sustainability with the sustainable recipes and information in this book. May you be blessed as you get back to the basics and enjoy your journey to the self-sustainable life.

Receive free sustainable articles on my website at
gameandgarden.com

Become a fan of my facebook page at
facebook.com/SustainableStacy

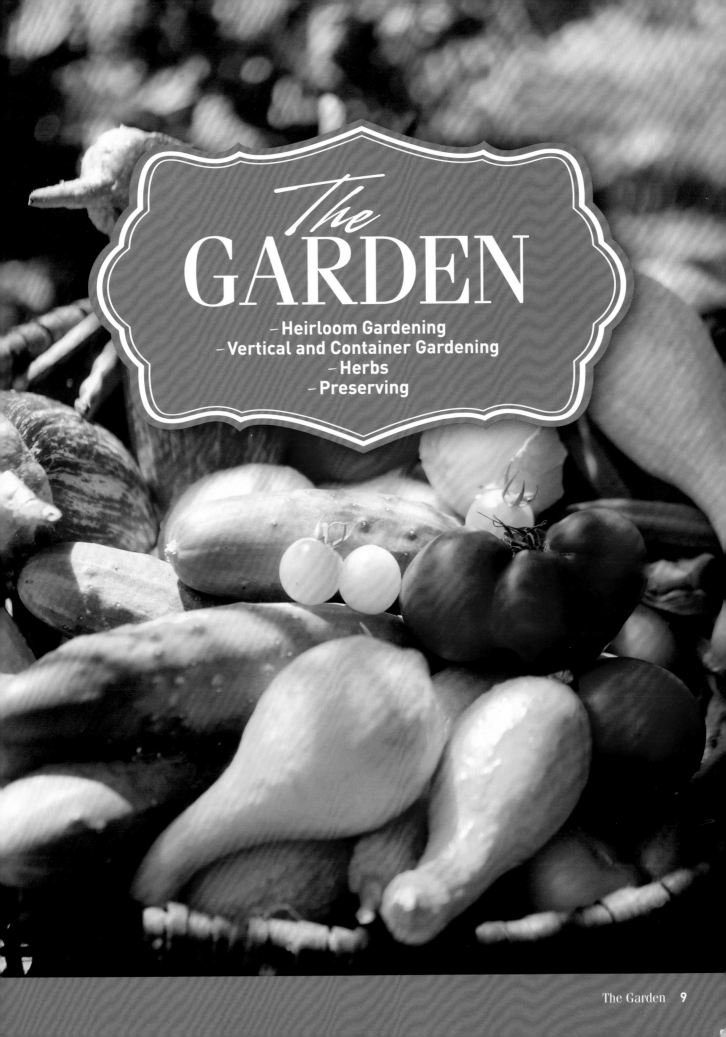

The GARDEN

- Heirloom Gardening
- Vertical and Container Gardening
- Herbs
- Preserving

Heirloom Gardening

History has given us many gifts, one of which is the continuation of plants using seeds dating back thousands of years. I love just dreaming of the life our ancestors lived and the gardens that they tended and nurtured. My family of nine makes a habit of visiting historic plantations in different states each year. The one commonality is that they all have a garden spot, whether it be a knot garden, square foot garden, or a huge planted garden. I love them all, as I am sure their owners have through the years.

More than the historical romanticism that I love so dearly, heirloom gardening affords very practical benefits. Many of the best-tasting, most prolific, healthy, and health-producing plants are harvested from heirloom seeds. Additionally, family unity and sustainability as well as being part of history, geography, science, and wildlife contribute to an abundance of living and fulfillment that very few activities can match.

Heirloom varieties are usually not as uniform in shape as hybrid plants, but the flavor is exceptional in comparison. We are used to seeing beautiful, perfect-looking specimens in the grocery store, therefore heirloom produce appears to be less attractive, but once you have tasted the captivating heirloom varieties, they become alluringly gorgeous because of what they contribute in flavor, texture, and their extraordinary uniqueness.

Because heirlooms have not been genetically modified, they are able to produce plants that are just as prolific, healthy, disease-resistant, and resilient to weather extremes as they did for our ancestors. Genetically modified plants have genes added or deleted from them, causing alterations in the entire structure of the plant. Genetic engineering is usually done to achieve a trait that is not normally held by an organism. These genetically modified plants bear sterile seeds or seeds that revert only to one of the parent genes, therefore never producing the same plant if producing a plant at all. Heirloom seeds are open-pollinating seeds, which mean that they can reproduce themselves from seeds. God created the cycle of plant life whereby a seed falls to the ground and the seed produces another plant in its likeness. Why disturb the perfect means of reproduction given by our Creator?

It is truly amazing that by planting heirloom seeds, we are planting a piece of history. Our own native Indians have provided us with the original corn, squash, and potatoes that they survived on. Many seeds traveled over the seas and were brought by European and Asian immigrants. The Europeans brought cabbage, pole beans, and carrots. The Asians brought radishes, lettuces, and onions. We are tasting the same flavors and textures as did our predecessors. History is being seen right in our flourishing heirloom gardens.

Family stories are connected to many of the heirloom seeds we possess. The seeds, just like the infamous family recipes, get passed down through the generations, along with the stories of our great-great grandmothers and grandfathers who harvested and cooked from these very plants and relied on them for their sustenance. My dad is passing the purple-hull peas that have adorned our table for as long as I remember down to me and my children. I am sure that our ancestors enjoyed family unity as I do with my children in the great outdoors, actually living life while sharing responsibility and passing down life-giving truths by teaching the necessities of life while working alongside of one another. These real activities of life give competence to the next generation and teach responsibility and care for the earth.

Heirloom seeds consistently yield a crop of fruits, vegetables, and herbs with extraordinary flavor, life-giving health, family unity, and life long sustainability. Our ancestors have always relied on their kitchen gardens as a way of life, and we should learn to do the same and pass down our knowledge and passion for generations to come. I look forward to passing down my favorite life-giving heirloom seeds and recipes to my children and children's children as well as to anyone else who will appreciate them.

Heirloom Gardening Tips

1. Always order seeds from a reputable source such as Rareseeds.com or Southernexposure.com

2. Be sure to get your soil tested in the winter to adjust the pH. Send your soil to your local extension office for results. This tip will save money and headaches.

3. Many seeds need a head start indoors. Try not to be too hasty to plant, because if plants are left indoors too long, they will become weak and lanky. It is best to move them outdoors when the plants produce their second set of leaves.

4. Be careful to acclimate the plants that have been indoors for a few days to a week on a porch or near the house in the shade before planting in the ground. This gives them a chance to get accustomed to the bright sun and temperature.

5. Keep a garden journal or layout of what you are planting and where you are planting so that the subsequent spring you can rotate your crops. This will improve soil structure and decrease the likelihood of pests.

6. When saving seeds, choose your most robust and favorite plants to extract the seeds. Always store seeds in a dry, cool, and dark location. I like to use 4-ounce glass Mason jars and store them in the refrigerator. The seeds should last for years.

Roasted Garden Vegetables

Serves 6

When I can no longer see my kitchen island for all the vegetables covering it, I know that it is time for Roasted Garden Vegetables. These vegetables pair well with any meat and are great on salads.

Ingredients

2 eggplants

2 cups cherry tomatoes or tomatoes cut in chunks

2 onions, quartered

Olive oil, for drizzling

2 tablespoons oregano

2 tablespoons basil

1 tablespoon kosher salt

1 tablespoon freshly ground pepper

1. Preheat oven to 450 degrees.

2. Roughly cut eggplants, onions, and tomatoes. Place vegetables in groups on sheet pan. Drizzle olive oil on top of vegetables. Do not crowd the pan or the vegetables will steam.

3. Sprinkle oregano, basil, salt, and pepper over vegetables and roast for 15 minutes. Turn each piece and roast for 5 to 10 minutes more. Sprinkle with extra salt if desired and serve.

Fried Squash with Tomatoes and Pesto

Serves 4

This is a fantastic meal for those days your garden harvest is packed full of squash. If you have some frozen pesto on hand, this is an especially quick and easy meal. I prefer to use my leftover tomato sauce from my meatless spaghetti in preparation for this recipe. This is also a great dish when entertaining because you can prepare the pesto and tomato sauce in advance and refrigerate for later usage. This dish is amazingly impressive in appearance and taste!

• You can substitute eggplant for squash in this recipe.

Ingredients

1 cup Basic Tomato Sauce (p. 22)
1 cup Basil Pesto (p. 52)
4 medium-sized squash
1 cup flour
1 teaspoon kosher salt

½ teaspoon pepper
2 eggs
1 tablespoon water
1 cup bread crumbs
Olive oil, for frying

4 tablespoons butter, for frying
2 tomatoes, sliced into ¼ inch slices
Basil leaves, for garnishing

1. Prepare tomato sauce and pesto.

2. Cut squash into ¼-inch slices lengthwise.

3. On a large plate, mix flour, salt, and pepper. On a second plate beat eggs and water together. Place bread crumbs on a third plate. Coat squash slices into seasoned flour, then egg mixture, then bread crumbs.

4. In a hot sauté pan, mix butter and oil. When sizzling, place coated slices in pan for about 2 to 3 minutes per side or until squash is tender. Cook in batches. Transfer to a platter and keep warm.

5. Place tablespoon of pesto in center of a plate and begin to layer fried squash, tomato sauce, tomato, and repeat beginning again with the pesto until you have at least 4 slices of squash. Garnish with a basil leaf.

Squash Boats

Serves 4

I love to eat these jewels as a meal in the summertime. This dish is light and refreshing after a long day in our hot, Alabama summers. It is also hearty and tasty enough to leave me satisfied.

Ingredients

4 yellow squash
3 tablespoons olive oil, divided
1 Vidalia onion, chopped
3 cloves garlic, chopped
2 tomatoes, chopped

1 teaspoon oregano, chopped
1 teaspoon basil, chopped
¾ cup bread crumbs, divided
¾ cup Parmesan cheese, divided
1 teaspoon kosher salt

½ teaspoon freshly ground pepper
2 eggs, beaten
4 tablespoons butter

1. Preheat oven to 350 degrees.

2. Halve squash lengthwise and scoop out the seeds and soft flesh with a spoon and discard. Place squash into a baking dish.

3. Heat 2 tablespoons of olive oil in a sauté pan over medium heat and sauté onions and garlic for about 5 minutes or until onions are translucent. Remove from heat. Add tomatoes and cook 2 minutes. Add oregano, ¼ cup bread crumbs, ¼ cup cheese, salt, pepper, and the eggs into the skillet and mix well.

4. Mound the stuffing into the cavity of the squash. Top the mounds with remaining bread crumbs and dot each with butter. Bake for 20-25 minutes or until mounds are golden brown and squash can be punctured easily with a fork.

5. Remove from oven, sprinkle remaining Parmesan cheese on top. Drizzle with remaining olive oil and garnish with basil.

Eggplant Lasagna

Serves 10

    This is an extremely healthful, low fat, full-of-flavor meal. The robust flavors of the tomato sauce and pesto paired with the saltiness of the ricotta will satisfy the heartiest of appetites.

Ingredients

3 tablespoons olive oil, plus more for sautéing

1 tablespoon fresh oregano, chopped

1 teaspoon salt

1 tablespoon fresh thyme, chopped

½ teaspoon kosher salt

½ teaspoon freshly ground pepper

3 medium eggplants

2 cups tomato sauce

2 cups ricotta cheese

Basil Pesto (p. 52)

2 cups mozzarella cheese, shredded

1. Preheat oven to 350 degrees.

2. Slice eggplant into ⅛ inch slices using a very sharp knife or mandolin.

3. In a large bowl mix olive oil, oregano, thyme, salt, and pepper. Toss eggplant in mixture.

4. Heat oil in a nonstick sauté pan over high heat. When oil is shimmering place eggplant and sauté until pliable.

5. Spoon about ½ cup tomato sauce on bottom of 9" x 11" baking dish. Place a layer of eggplant then more tomato sauce. Dollop ricotta and pesto using about ⅓ of each ingredient. Add another layer of eggplant slices and repeat twice more with the tomato, ricotta, and pesto. Top with mozzarella cheese.

6. Bake for 35 to 40 minutes or until cheese is bubbly and lightly browned.

Eggplant Lasagna

Collards

Serves 8

Collard greens are an all-time favorite in the South. They pair well with just about any protein or a well-balanced vegetable plate. My mom loves to eat a big bowl of these earthy greens with crumbled jalapeno cornbread for a very satisfying meal. If you ever try it this way, you will be hooked for life!

HINT: Soak the entire bunch of leaves in water for about 30 minutes then rinse the greens in running water for about 3 minutes before cooking fresh collards.

• Collard greens are loaded with vitamin K, which helps with increasing bone mass and decreases the effects of Alzheimer's disease by limiting neuronal damage.

• Sweating means to cook vegetables in a little fat over low heat. This process releases the moisture in the vegetables, not browns them. Sweating is different than caramelizing vegetables in that you cook vegetables in fat over low heat until they are brown. This process releases moisture and develops a nutty, sweet flavor in the vegetables, notably onions.

Ingredients

Olive oil

1 onion , chopped

1 tablespoon garlic

2 pounds collards, washed and pulled from the stem

2 cups white wine

4 cups broth

¼ teaspoon red pepper flakes

1 tablespoon kosher salt

¼ teaspoon freshly ground pepper

1. Heat olive oil in a large sauté pan over medium heat. Sweat the onions until they are translucent, about 10 minutes. Add garlic and continue to cook for 30 seconds longer.

2. Place washed collards into sauté pan. You may have to add half of the greens to the pan and let them shrink and then add the other half. Add wine, broth, red pepper flakes, salt, and pepper to the pan. Bring mixture to a boil and lower to simmer for 1 hour.

Creamed Brussels Sprouts

Serves 6

When I mention Brussels sprouts most everyone I know contorts their face in such a way that demonstrates disgust until they try this recipe. People who have hated Brussels sprouts their entire lives admit them to now be one of their beloved vegetables. My kids eat them like candy!

Ingredients

1 quart Brussels sprouts

2 tablespoons butter, melted

¾ cup boiling whipping cream

Salt and pepper

1. Preheat oven to 350 degrees.

2. Trim stem and outer layer of the Brussels sprouts.

3. In a stock pot, blanch sprouts for 3 minutes in boiling water. Drain and place sprouts in a casserole arranged in a single layer.

4. Pour butter over sprouts and sprinkle with salt and pepper. Place in oven for 10 minutes.

5. Pour cream over sprouts and bake for 10 more minutes or until sprouts are tender. Season as desired and serve as soon as possible.

Tomatoes

To say that our family loves tomatoes is an understatement. We love to can, dry, freeze them; eat them in sauces, on pasta, salads, and especially eat the fabulously simple tomato sandwich. Tomatoes make everything taste great. It is crazy to think that these tasty creations were once considered poisonous by Europeans! Boy, did they ever miss out?

Each year we have been planting different heirloom varieties and having a family taste test to judge which variety is best. We have planted Chocolate Stripe, Brandywine, Bonnie's Best, Paste tomatoes, and several cherry tomato varieties. The all-around favorite was Bonnie's Best tomato. Bonnie's Best Heirloom was created at the turn of the century in Union Springs, Alabama. Although Bonnie's Best won, all of them have winning qualities. For instance, the Chocolate Stripe is incredibly beautiful adorned with green and red stripes vertically around the entire tomato and the Brandywine is succulently sweet and juicy. We plan on crossing a few generations of these tomato plants and experimenting with making our own variety.

Saving Tomato Seeds

Saving seeds from tomatoes is a little different than saving seeds from most vegetables. It is not hard at all, but a little more time consuming and VERY worth it. I like to save seeds from at least three tomatoes from each variety. Complete the following steps separately for each variety. Our family of nine needs about one-hundred tomato plants to have canned tomatoes throughout the winter, therefore we save at least one-hundred seeds.

• Even though there has been controversy as to which category tomatoes belong, whether fruit or vegetable, the Supreme Court ruled that tomatoes are a vegetable for import purposes.

1. Harvest seeds from your favorite, healthiest tomato plant.
2. Cut the fruit in half. Squeeze the seeds into a clean container. Double the volume of liquid by adding equal parts pure water.
3. Let the tomatoes ferment in a warm, faraway place (they stink!) for three days or until a scum forms on the top. Add more water and stir.
4. Pour water off of the top, discarding the seeds that float. The good seeds will drop to the bottom of the container. Repeat until only good seeds remain.
5. Transfer seeds into a strainer and dry with a towel. Place seeds on a clean plate until completely dry.
6. Store seeds in a small glass jar in a cool, dark place.

Tomato Soup

Serves 4-6

    I remember as a child thinking, who would eat tomato soup? My only memory is my mother opening a can and enjoying this red soup. If I had been introduced to fresh-ripe tomato soup I think this memory would be much different. I dream of eating this scrumptious soup from the time I plant the tomatoes in the ground.

• Tomatoes are considered one of the most heart-healthy foods. Fresh tomatoes help lower cholesterol and triglycerides. They are also a great source of lycopene, which is known for its incredible antioxidant properties and aid in bone health.

Ingredients

3 pounds tomatoes

2 tablespoons butter

1 onion, chopped

2 carrots, chopped

1 cup vegetable stock

½ teaspoon basil, chopped

½ teaspoon oregano, chopped

Salt and pepper to taste

⅓ heavy cream, optional

1. Preheat oven to 450 degrees. Stem and halve tomatoes lengthwise, and then place tomatoes cut-side down on a lined cookie sheet and roast for 10 minutes. When tomatoes are cool enough to handle, remove skin and set aside.

2. Melt butter in heavy-bottomed stockpot. Add onion and carrots. Cook until soft.

3. Stir in tomatoes, stock, basil, and oregano. Bring to a boil, and then lower the heat to simmer. Cover pot and keep at simmer for about 20 minutes.

4. Carefully transfer mixture to a food processor and purée. Salt and pepper to taste.

SERVING SUGGESTION: Warm tomato soup in a saucepan. Stir ⅓ cup of heavy cream into soup and bring to a boil.

Basic Tomato Sauce

Yields one quart

Ingredients

5 tablespoons olive oil

1 large onion, diced

1 clove garlic, finely chopped

1 lb. tomatoes, fresh or canned, peeled, and chopped with their juices

1 teaspoon salt

½ teaspoon pepper

3 basil leaves, chopped

1. Heat the oil in medium sauce pan. Add onions and cook over low to medium heat until translucent. Approximately 6 minutes.

2. Stir in garlic, tomatoes, salt, pepper, and basil. Cook for 30 minutes.

3. With immersion blender or food processor purée tomato mixture.

Adjust seasonings. Serve.

Roasted Heirloom Cherry Tomatoes

Serves 4

Cherry tomatoes are the perfect side dish for any meal, breakfast, brunch, lunch, or dinner. I have friends who eat them like candy straight from the plant as snacks. Cherry tomatoes range from bright yellow and red to orange and pink and come in a variety of shapes and sizes. The color and shape alone add texture and visual appeal to any main course.

HINT: Fresh cherry tomatoes will work in this recipe, but heirloom varieties taste much sweeter.

• Vegetables and fruits of all shades contain phytonutrients including carotenoids and anthocyanin that produce the color in foods and help to protect your body. Choose colorful vegetables and fruits and stay healthy!

Ingredients

2 cups heirloom cherry tomatoes

¼ olive oil

2 tablespoons balsamic vinegar

1 tablespoon basil plus extra for garnish, chopped

1 tablespoon oregano plus extra for garnish, chopped

1 teaspoon salt

½ teaspoon pepper

½ cup Parmesan cheese (optional)

1. Preheat oven to 400 degrees.

2. In a medium bowl, mix together tomatoes, olive oil, balsamic vinegar, basil, oregano, salt, and pepper.

3. Pour tomatoes onto a lined cookie sheet and place in oven for 10-12 minutes or until tomatoes caramelize.

4. Place tomatoes on a serving dish and garnish with basil and oregano. Sprinkle with Parmesan cheese. Serve warm.

Roasted Heirloom Cherry Tomatoes

Tomato Pie

Serves 8

I have fond memories of this pie. My grandfather had four brothers and one sister who were very close. Every year they and their children and grandchildren would meet at Orange Beach, Alabama, where my great aunts would cook massive amounts of food. Amazingly, one of my favorite dishes was Tomato Pie. Once you try it, you'll understand why!

Ingredients

1 homemade pie crust, (p. 25)

3 tablespoons mayonnaise

¾ cup dry breadcrumbs

2½ pounds heirloom tomatoes, thinly sliced

2 Vidalia onions, thinly sliced

1 teaspoon salt

½ teaspoon pepper

2 tablespoons basil, chopped

1 tablespoon oregano, chopped

½ cup aged cheddar cheese, shredded

½ cup mozzarella cheese, shredded

¼ cup Parmesan cheese, grated, plus more for sprinkling

2 tablespoons olive oil, plus more for drizzling

1. Roll pie crust to fit a 10-inch deep pie plate. Place crust into plate and refrigerate for 30 minutes.

2. Preheat oven to 375 degrees.

3. Remove pie crust from refrigerator and cover lightly with aluminum foil. Place dried beans on top of the foil and bake for 12 minutes. Remove foil and beans and return crust back into the oven for another 4-5 minutes or until crust is golden in color. Remove and place on cooling rack. Lightly brush mayonnaise on surface of crust and let cool completely.

4. Sprinkle ¼ of breadcrumbs over bottom of crust. Layer half of the tomatoes, onions, salt, pepper, basil, oregano, cheddar cheese, mozzarella cheese, and Parmesan cheese. Repeat with another ¼ cup of breadcrumbs and remaining tomatoes, onions, salt, pepper, basil, oregano, and cheeses.

5. In a small bowl, combine olive oil and remaining breadcrumbs. Sprinkle breadcrumbs on top of tomato pie and finish with another drizzle of olive oil.

6. Bake the pie for about 1 hour or until hot and bubbly. Remove pie from oven and sprinkle with Parmesan cheese. Let pie cool for an hour and serve.

Homemade Pie Crust

Yields 2, 10-inch pie crusts

Ingredients

3 cups all- purpose flour

1 teaspoon kosher salt

¾ cups unsalted butter (1 ½ sticks), very cold

⅓ cup vegetable shortening (Crisco), very cold

6 tablespoons ice water, plus more if dough is too thick

1. Place flour and salt into food processor fitted with a steel blade and pulse to mix.

2. Dice butter. Add diced butter and cold shortening to processor.

3. Add ice water to the mixture down the feed tube with machine running. Pulse machine until dough forms a ball. Wrap in plastic wrap. Refrigerate 30 minutes.

4. Cut dough in half. Roll one of the pieces on a well-floured board, rolling from the center to the edge, turning and flouring the dough to make sure it does not stick.

5. Continue rolling until 14 inches in diameter. Fold the dough in half over the rolling pin, place in pie plate. Unfold and mold to pie plate.

6. If making a double-crusted pie, roll remaining half of dough out on a well-floured surface. Roll from the center to the edge, turning, flouring, and rolling until you get a disc with the diameter of approximately 12 inches or to desired size. Using a sharp knife, trim the edges of the top crust leaving a ¾-inch overhang under the original pie crust and crimp the edges using your index finger and thumb. Make steam vents by using a sharp knife to cut 4 slits in center of top crust.

7. If making a lattice crust, roll remaining half of dough into an 8 X 10-inch rectangle about ⅛ inch thick. Cut the rectangle lengthwise into 1-inch strips. Make sure to do this on a floured surface so lattice strips do not stick. Place strips about one inch apart over top of pie. Fold back every other strip halfway over itself and place one of the remaining strips perpendicular to the original. Return the strips that had been folded back to their original position. Fold back the alternate strips and place another strip across the unfolded strips. Return strips that are folded back to the original position and repeat by continuing to weave the lattice on top of the pie filling. Roll the overhang under bottom pie crust. Use a sharp knife to trim off the excess. Use your index finger and thumb to pinch dough to make a fluted design.

Dandelion Greens, Arugula, and Crispy Fried Goat Cheese

Serves 4

In our family we have a tradition of taking one of our children out every week. On one of these trips we went to a farm-to-table restaurant where we had this absolutely awesome salad packed full of flavor. I wanted to replicate the salad, but with a few improvements.

HINT: When slicing goat cheese, wipe your knife with a warm wet towel. If your slices crumble just use your finger to mold them back together.

• Panko can be found in most grocery stores and is made with white bread without the crust. They give extra crunch, but regular bread crumb will do just fine for this recipe.

Ingredients

2 cups dandelion greens

2 cups spinach leaves

2 cups arugula

½ cup tomatoes, roughly chopped

16 oz. goat cheese

2 eggs, beaten

1 cup Panko breadcrumbs

2 teaspoons diced parsley

1 teaspoon diced thyme

1 pinch salt

½ teaspoon freshly ground black pepper

½ cup flour

Olive oil for frying

Tomato Vinaigrette (below)

1. Place goat cheese log in freezer for 15 minutes to make it easier to slice.

2. Place flour into a shallow dish or plate. In a second shallow dish, beat eggs. In a third dish, stir Panko, parsley, thyme, salt, and pepper until combined.

3. Remove cheese from freezer and slice into ½-inch rounds.

4. Coat cheese in flour, then egg mixture, then Panko mixture. Repeat with remaining cheese and set aside.

5. In a non-stick sauté pan, place just enough oil to cover the bottom. Heat oil on high heat. Once oil is shimmering, place coated cheese in pan for about 1 to 2 minutes. Do not crowd the pan or it will steam instead of fry. Turn cheese over and cook for another minute or until cheese is golden. Remove cheese from pan and transfer to a paper towel. Repeat with remaining cheese.

6. Meanwhile, in a large bowl, mix dandelions, spinach, arugula and tomatoes. Spoon 4 tablespoons of Tomato Vinaigrette and toss gently.

7. Divide salad mix onto 4 plates. Divide fried cheese among the plates and drizzle extra Tomato Vinaigrette as desired. Serve immediately.

Tomato Vinaigrette

Yields about ¾ cup

Ingredients

2 tablespoons salad vinegar

1 teaspoon sugar

½ shallot, minced

1 clove garlic, minced

½ teaspoon kosher salt

¼ teaspoon pepper

1 ripe tomato, blanched and peeled

¼ cup olive oil

Place all ingredients in a food processor and pour oil in a stream slowly. Blend continually until emulsified.

Dandelion Greens, Arugula, and Crispy Fried Goat Cheese

Roasted Okra

Serves 4 to 6

Okra is a "love it" or "hate it" kind of vegetable. I think it is all in the preparation just like most ingredients. People do not like it in that it can become very slimy, but if made correctly, you can have the flavor without the slime. In the South, it is a "must have" in soups and gumbo. In the preparation for this recipe, the okra has a little heat and is slightly crunchy on the outside. Make sure you pick your okra or choose okra from the farmer's market or store that is no more than 3 inches long. The smaller the okra, the more tender the bite.

Ingredients

1 pound young okra (less than 3 inches)

¼ cup olive oil

1½ tablespoons cumin

1½ teaspoon salt

1 teaspoon black pepper

½ teaspoon chipotle chili pepper

1. Preheat oven to 400 degrees.

2. Toss okra in olive oil to coat. Combine all dry spices and toss with okra.

3. Place okra onto a sheet pan in a single layer.

4. Bake for 5-7 minutes and turn okra over onto the other side. Bake for another 3-5 minutes or until pods are softened.

Butter Beans

Serves 8

A vegetable plate is a favorite in our household, and especially at the beginning of harvest season. A vegetable plate is just not complete without some type of beans such as crowder peas, black-eyed peas, or butter beans. It has always been a favorite family tradition to spend the afternoon on the porch shelling peas to "put up" for the winter. Now with our big family, the peas rarely make it to the "put up" stage, but nonetheless, shelling peas is timeless and is enjoyed by every generation and should be a time for celebration!

Ingredients

2 tablespoons olive oil

½ cup Vidalia onion, chopped

1 clove garlic, minced

1 pound butter beans

2 okra, whole

4 cups chicken stock

1 teaspoon kosher salt

¼ teaspoon freshly ground pepper

½ lemon, juiced

1 tablespoon butter

3 tablespoons sliced green onion tops (green part)

1. Heat olive oil in medium saucepan over medium high heat. Add the onions and reduce heat to medium until onions are translucent. Add the garlic and cook for 1 minute.

2. Add the beans, okra, stock, salt, pepper, lemon juice and butter. Bring to a boil. Reduce the heat and simmer for 25-30 minutes or until the beans are tender. Be careful to keep an eye on the beans. Add water if they look dry. Season as desired. Serve with sliced green onions.

Corn

Throughout my entire life I have heard stories from my Granny's perspective of my appetite being only desirous of corn products when feasting at her home. She told of the dissension between herself and my parents over this issue. With such a wide array of healthy food, my choice was only limited to sweet corn and she understood this perfectly. She and I could not understand why my parents were not on board with this!

Sweet corn. What could be better? Over 70 percent of American processed foods contain some form of genetically modified ingredients mostly consisting of corn. That can be quite disturbing considering that the domesticated varieties used by the corporate farmers selling to the manufacturers contain Genetically Modified Organisms. These domesticated varieties cannot survive without the aid of humans. How bizarre? Thankfully, we can plant heirloom varieties. My favorite is Country Gentleman, a shoepeg variety of corn. It is a fine specimen. It needs to be cooked at once after picking it in that it begins losing its sugar content only a few minutes after it is picked from the stalk.

If you desire to save the seeds for next year's planting, beware of any neighboring farms growing hybrid corn. If the neighboring corn field is within a one to two mile radius, it will cross pollinate and your corn may then be subject to Genetically Modified Organisms.

HINT: Plant a flint variety of corn for grinding corn meal.

Corn Chowder

Serves 10-12

Corn chowder always reminds me of one of my husband's best friends. He raves about my recipe and I think the secret to its success is the use of fresh corn. Although frozen corn is certainly acceptable, the fresh corn pops in your mouth and adds a special sweetness that is exceptional. I personally think the white cheddar cheese in the recipe gives this dish its wow factor, but this friend, whose name I can't disclose, is "allergic" to cheese. That's code for "I hate cheese;" therefore I make that optional in the recipe.

Ingredients

8 strips bacon, diced
2 large onions, chopped
⅓ cup flour
8 cups chicken stock

8 cups chopped potatoes
1 teaspoon salt
½ teaspoon pepper
8 ears fresh or 4 cups frozen corn

2 cups light cream (half and half)
1 tomato, diced
8 ounces sharp white cheddar cheese, optional

1. Sauté bacon and onion in heavy-bottom stock pot. Drain excess fat.

2. Sprinkle flour on top of onion and bacon mixture. Pour chicken stock, potatoes, salt, and pepper into pot and bring to a boil. Reduce to simmer for 15-20 minutes or until potatoes are tender.

3. Meanwhile, boil corn for 3-5 minutes. Drain and cut corn off the cob.

4. Add corn and cream into pot and heat through. Ladle into bowl and serve with tomatoes and, if desired, cheese.

Corn Chowder

Creamy Corn Pudding

Serves 4

This corn pudding is one of my all-time favorites for Christmas meals or alongside a BIG barbecue sandwich. It's one of the most versatile dishes I know. As a 5-year-old, this was the only dish I would eat when I went to my grandmother's house. This, however, caused a lot of tension. My parents wanted me to eat a variety of foods and my granny wanted me to have "whatever the darling wants"!

HINT: You can use canned creamed corn as a substitute for the fresh or frozen corn.

• To remove silk from corn use a wet paper towel.

• When buying corn from the market, pick the ears with husks bright green, and the kernels full and milky.

Ingredients

4 tablespoons melted butter, divided

¼ cup bell peppers, diced

¼ cup onions, diced

2 tablespoons flour

½ teaspoon salt

¼ cup sugar

2 cups corn (fresh or frozen) Note: If using fresh corn, boil corn (on cob) for 3 minutes before cutting off the kernels. Try to scrape all the milk from the corn as you work.

4 eggs, beaten

1 ⅓ cup milk (for extra creamy pudding, replace the milk with half and half)

1. Preheat oven to 325 degrees.

2. In a large sauté pan, sauté bell peppers and onions in 2 tablespoons of butter.

3. In a large bowl, mix flour, salt, sugar, and corn.

4. Add eggs, milk, remaining butter, and sautéed vegetables. Pour mixture into casserole. Place in a roasting pan and pour water halfway up the casserole.

5. Bake 45 minutes or until pudding is golden brown.

Jalapeno Cornbread

Serves 6

This cornbread is great with just about anything, but especially soups and chili. The corn kernels give the cornbread extra texture that complements any dish.

- If you are having a large crowd, you can double the recipe. You may have to leave it in the oven a little longer than this recipe calls for. To check for doneness, stick a toothpick into the center of the cornbread. If it comes out clean and the top is golden brown, it is ready.

Ingredients

¼ cup bacon drippings (or the same amount of a vegetable oil)

½ cup buttermilk

½ cup sour cream

2 large eggs, beaten

½ cup corn, fresh or frozen

1 jalapeno chile, minced and seeded

1 cup cornmeal

1½ teaspoons baking powder

½ teaspoon baking soda

½ teaspoon salt

1. Preheat oven to 400 degrees.

2. In oven, heat drippings in a 9-inch skillet until sizzling hot.

3. Meanwhile, combine sour cream, buttermilk, eggs, corn, and chile in large bowl. Stir in cornmeal, baking powder, baking soda, and salt.

4. Pour drippings from skillet into cornbread mixture and mix well. The drippings should sizzle when they hit the batter. Pour batter into skillet.

5. Bake for 30 minutes or until golden brown.

Garlic Mashed Potatoes

Serves 8

   Mashed potatoes are the ultimate comfort food that accompanies just about any dish. The added garlic gives these perfectly mashed potatoes that extra punch that brings an ordinary meal up a notch.

HINT: To avoid gummy potatoes, only add warm ingredients to the potatoes (warm butter and cream) and drain potatoes completely removing as much water as possible.

• Potatoes grow from pieces of potatoes or whole potatoes planted in rich soil. The tubers will grow underground. Once the plant blooms and you see it flower, the potatoes are ready to harvest.

Ingredients

4 pounds Idaho potatoes, peeled and
   cut into 1 inch pieces
½ cup butter, melted
1 cup half and half, warmed
1 cup heavy cream, warmed
6 garlic cloves, finely minced
Kosher salt
Freshly ground black pepper

1. Place potatoes in a large Dutch oven. Cover potatoes with salted water and bring to a boil. Reduce heat to medium and cook potatoes until tender, about 15 minutes. Remove from heat and drain. Return potatoes to pot and place back on stove.

2. With a potato masher, slowly integrate the butter and half and half. Add the heavy cream and garlic and mix in with an electric mixer on medium speed until smooth. If potatoes are too stiff add more cream. Add salt and pepper to taste.

Sweet Potatoes

The first year my family attempted to grow sweet potatoes, we waited and waited for the leaves to arrive on the plant. Every day we checked the plants and the stems seemed to be at a standstill with no leaves. The poor grasslike stems looked as if they had been freshly mowed with a lawn mower. I could not sleep one night and began looking out the window at 3 A.M., and I finally had the answer to the "root" of the problem; a doe and three fawns! We learned quickly to protect these obviously luscious plants from the hungry deer.

Sweet potatoes will last for up to six months if cured and stored properly. The natural sweetness of sweet potatoes improves with proper curing. Store sweet potatoes at around 85 degrees for 10 days. I use my back porch in that Alabama remains hot during the sweet potato harvest season. After the curing process, move the sweet potatoes to a storage place such as a basement or root cellar kept between 55 and 60 degrees.

Mashed Sweet Potatoes

Serves 6

You can't go wrong serving sweet potatoes with steak, quail, venison, and some fish dishes. Not only are they a healthy choice, they bring an earthy quality that gives a subtle comfort. The Southerner's garden would not be complete without this perfect root vegetable.

• Nature's perfect beauty food? Sweet potatoes contain twice as much fiber as the other potatoes and are full of vitamins B6, A, C, and E. These nutrients contribute to a glowing complexion and vibrantly healthy hair.

Ingredients

3 pounds sweet potatoes, peeled and cut into chunks

4 tablespoons (½ stick) butter

½ cup packed brown sugar

½ teaspoon nutmeg

Salt and pepper to taste

1. Place potatoes in large pot and add water to just cover them. Set heat to high and boil potatoes until tender, and then drain.

2. Place potatoes back into the pot and fold in butter and sugar until dissolved. Blend in spices with a hand mixer until well incorporated and potatoes are smooth. Serve hot with extra butter!

Sweet Potato Baked Fries

Serves 4 to 6

   I often eat these all-around winner fries as a meal. The savory fries are great piled up under venison or organic beef steak, and the sweeter version, Cinnamon Sugar Sweet Potato Fries, are perfect as a dessert. Surprisingly, both the savory and sweet fries are delicious with the Chipotle Dipping Sauce.

• You may be tempted to skip boiling the potatoes, but this step helps the potatoes to be crispy on the outside and tender on the inside. It is well worth it!

Ingredients

2 pounds potatoes, cut into ½-inch
   strips (fries)

3 tablespoons olive oil
1 tablespoon cumin

½ teaspoon salt
¼ teaspoon cayenne pepper

1. Preheat oven to 425 degrees.

2. Bring a large stockpot of water to a boil. Place potatoes in pot and boil for about 6-8 minutes or until al dente.

3. Drain potatoes and then dry with paper towels.

4. Mix remaining ingredients in medium-sized bowl. Place potatoes in the mixture and coat evenly.

5. Spread sweet potatoes on a cookie sheet. Use two cookie sheets if potatoes are touching, or potatoes will steam instead of bake.

6. Place potatoes in oven for 30 minutes or until golden and crispy, turning them occasionally.

7. Remove and serve with Chipotle Dipping Sauce.

Chipotle Dipping Sauce

• If you want to cheat on the homemade mayonnaise, use Hellman's mayonnaise.

1 cup Homemade Mayonnaise (p. 90)
1 ripe (red) jalapeno

½ lemon, juiced
Pinch of salt

1. Heat a cast iron skillet to smoking hot. Place jalapeno on skillet and cover with lid or pan to create roasting effect. Rotate pepper occasionally (once a minute), until all sides are charred. Remove stem and skin from pepper.

2. Place pepper along with the rest of the ingredients into a food processor and blend until smooth. Check seasoning and serve.

Cinnamon Sugar Sweet Potato Fries

Replace the dry ingredients with ¼ cup sugar, 1 tablespoon cinnamon, and ¼ teaspoon nutmeg and continue with recipe instructions for the Sweet Potato Baked Fries.

Poached Pears

Poached Pears

Serves 6

I once was told that poached pears were a favorite in Italy, and I know they are a favorite around here. I love to make these beauties for breakfast as well as serve them as a lovely dessert.

- Different pears will cook at different rates depending on size, type, and ripeness. You will know they are done when a knife pierces easily into the pear.

- To keep pears from discoloring, they must be basted frequently. It helps to have the pears fit snugly together.

Ingredients

Butter, for greasing casserole

6 ripe pears

1 cup orange juice

1 cup water

¼ cup of honey

½ teaspoon vanilla extract

⅛ teaspoon ground cinnamon

Zest of 1 orange

Freshly grated nutmeg (optional)

1. Preheat oven to 375 degrees. Butter a casserole just large enough to hold the pears.

2. Peel pears leaving stems. Slice bottom of pears flat so they stands upright. With a melon baller, scoop out the inside of pears through the bottom and remove seeds. Stand pears upright in casserole.

3. Add orange juice and water to the casserole and bake the pears for about 40 minutes or until you can pierce with a fork easily. Baste.

4. Transfer pears to a plate. Leave the oven on. Pour juices into a bowl and add honey, cinnamon, vanilla, and orange zest. Mix well. Place pears back into casserole and drizzle honey mixture over pears. You may not need all the mixture. Place pears back into the oven for 5 more minutes.

5. Stand a pear in a bowl. If you desire, sprinkle freshly grated nutmeg over the pears. Garnish with mint leaves. Serve with the honey mixture and your favorite chocolate sauce and whipped cream.

Perfect Peach Smoothie

Serves 4

There is nothing like eating a peach right off the tree, but I also love making this sweet treat for my family when our peach trees are full of ripe fruit. One little trick I love is using Greek yogurt in my smoothies. Greek yogurt is more tangy and creamier than your average yogurt. It has been strained of whey, lactose, and sugar, making the yogurt thicker and higher in protein. These characteristics along with the vitamin C from the peaches make for a great afternoon snack or healthy breakfast. Try it for yourself. You won't be disappointed!

Ingredients

2½ cups Greek yogurt

2 pounds peaches, peeled, pitted and chopped

½ cup honey

½ teaspoon vanilla extract

Ice cubes (about 10)

1. Place all ingredients in a food processor. Process while adding ice cubes one at a time until thick and smooth. Pour the mixture into four glasses or Mason jars. Enjoy!

Figs

It is amazing how food evokes such memories. My first and most precious remembrance of figs is eating them while sitting in the top of my granny's fig tree right after doing flips off the bars holding up her clothes line. Every year she would cut the tree right to the ground and I would be shocked to find a larger tree in its place the following year.

Fig trees have been mentioned from the days of Adam and Eve (Genesis 3:7). Throughout the ages figs have been a daily staple for the Hebrews, Egyptians, Cretans, and Romans. Figs are one of the Israelites' top seven traditional foods and have always symbolized wealth and prosperity in their culture. The Spaniards brought this amazing fruit to America in the 1600s and it remains today as one of the world's healthiest ingredients.

Both the fruit and the leaves hold healing and preventative powers. The fruit, fresh or dried, contains one of the highest amounts of fiber, aiding in weight loss and preventing post-menopausal breast cancer as well as having a high percentage of potassium which helps control blood pressure. The leaves are known to contain anti-diabetic properties that will reduce the amount of insulin diabetic patients require. The leaves have also been known to slow cancer cells' growth considerably.

Figs pair beautifully with meats, especially that of quail and fish. I love to serve fish steamed in a fig leaf with various herbs. Figs are extremely perishable and need to be eaten within a day of picking or purchasing. If you have figs available, take the opportunity to dry any unused figs and eat them as a snack or rehydrate them when you are ready to cook with them (p. 61).

Fig Bread

Yields 1 Loaf

This bread is a favorite in my family. My little ones love mashing up the figs and I love having their helping hands in the kitchen. The reward of eating this yummy, sweet bread isn't that bad either.

Ingredients

2 cups all purpose flour
1 ½ teaspoons baking soda
½ teaspoons salt

2 large eggs
½ teaspoon vanilla extract
½ cup butter room temperature, plus more for preparing pan

1 cup sugar, plus 3 tablespoons for seasoning pan
1 cup ripe figs
½ cup chopped pecans

1. Preheat oven to 350 degrees.

2. Stir the flour, baking soda and salt into a medium bowl and set aside.

3. In a separate bowl, whisk the eggs and vanilla extract together and set aside.

4. Butter a 9" × 5" × 3" loaf pan. Sprinkle 3 tablespoons of sugar in the bottom of the pan. Set aside.

5. In a large bowl use an electric hand mixer to cream the butter and sugar until light and fluffy. Slowly pour the egg mixture into the butter while mixing continuously.

6. Mix dry ingredients into the batter until just incorporated.

7. Mash figs with a fork so that they still have texture. Add figs to the mixture. Fold in the nuts. Pour the batter into pan. Bake for 1 hour and 15 minutes or until toothpick comes out clean.

8. Cool the bread on a wire rack for 10 minutes. Slice and serve.

Fig Bread

Figs Stuffed With Mascarpone and Maple Walnut

Serves 6 to 8

Figs are luscious served savory or sweet. There seems to be a magical quality about this amazingly adaptable fruit. When stuffed with mascarpone, the dish becomes velvety and then the crunch of the maple walnuts makes this dish sing.

Ingredients

16 figs

4 ounces cream cheese

4 ounces mascarpone cheese

1 tablespoon parsley, chopped

1 tablespoon honey, plus more for drizzling

1 ounces (¼ cup) chopped walnuts

1. Preheat oven to 350 degrees.

2. Cross the top half of the figs with a paring knife, dividing the stem base into fourths.

3. Mix cream cheese, mascarpone, parsley, honey, and 1 ounce of walnuts in a medium bowl until smooth. Stuff about a teaspoon of the mixture into each fig. Place figs on cookie sheet and bake for about 10 minutes.

4. Prepare maple walnuts. Drizzle with honey and serve warm.

Candied Maple Walnuts

Yields 1 Cup

Want a perfect topping? The combination of walnuts, maple syrup, and salt is your answer. I usually make a double batch because they are so good. I sometimes eat the topping before it makes it to its intended destination.

Ingredients

4 ounces (1 cup) walnuts, chopped

¼ cup maple syrup

Pinch of salt

1. Sauté walnuts in maple syrup for about 3 to 5 minutes or until the syrup begins to turn color and the nuts are toasted. Watch closely as you sauté because caramelizing is one step away from burning.

2. Remove walnuts from heat and place on a sheet of wax paper and let cool completely.

3. Use immediately or store in an airtight container for up to 2 weeks.

Cantaloupe Ice Cream

Yields about 6 cups

Cantaloupe grew profusely in our garden this year so we decided to try a few experimental recipes. This recipe ended up being a real "keeper." Scott said it was his favorite ice cream EVER! Now that is something to remember.

• Cantaloupe is known to help those who have insomnia by reducing the body's heart rate and reducing stress, thereby helping you to relax.

Ingredients

2 cups peeled and cubed cantaloupe

⅚ cup granulated sugar, divided (⅓ cup and ½ cup)

1½ tablespoons fresh lime juice

1¾ cups half and half

1¼ cup coconut milk

1. In a large bowl, combine the cubed cantaloupe with ⅓ cup of sugar. Cover and marinate at least 6 hours in the refrigerator.

2. In a saucepan over medium-low heat, simmer the marinated cantaloupe pieces in the juices of the marinade. Cook for 5 minutes, stirring occasionally, then remove and cool.

3. Purée the cantaloupe mixture in a blender or food processor. Add the lime juice and process again. Cover and chill for an hour.

4. In a large bowl, combine the half and half and coconut milk with the remaining ½ cup of sugar. Stir in the puréed cantaloupe, stirring gently to mix in.

5. Place mixture in the freezer for about 2 hours. Transfer to an ice cream maker and proceed with the manufacturer's instructions for making ice cream.

6. Place the cantaloupe ice cream into an airtight container and return to freezer for 2 hours before serving.

Vertical and Container Gardening

There should be nothing that holds you back from gardening. Do you have limited space or time? Is your house situated on a small lot, or do you live in an apartment? Vertical and container gardens are two fantastic ways to manage your favorite fruits, vegetables, and herbs in a small space and yield produce as if you had a large space. Container gardening is a perfect way to teach your little ones how to care for and nurture a garden as well as to build confidence.

Vertical gardening has many advantages and is used in large gardens as well as small gardens. Not only does it save space, the plant becomes less prone to pests and disease because the plant is off the ground. Plants use less water when grown vertically as well as shade herbs and vegetables that need a little less sun. The best plants to grow vertically are cucumbers, green beans, and peas. I also like to plant vertically in containers by planting cherry tomatoes, surrounded by basil, oregano, thyme and other Italian herbs.

A trellis can be built easily by using fallen limbs and tying them together in the shape of a tepee or by simply using a lattice board, giving plants a place to climb. When building your vertical structure, make sure your structure can support the weight of the vine and plants. One of my friends has a cucumber trellis on her porch to block an unsightly view. These trellises can also be planted on porches to give you more privacy.

I love walking by my beautiful yet functional container gardens! Not only are they gorgeous, I get the same amount of produce as if using a square foot of garden space. Using containers is inexpensive and less time-consuming in that you have the soil ready year after year with only having to amend the nutrients in the soil a little before each growing season. Bird baths, half of a wooden rain barrel, or old fountains make great unusual containers.

Even if you choose to plant only a few plants in a pot, you will be rewarded!

To Soak or Not to Soak

"Take your time" has never been a phrase that my mind has grasped very well. I pretty much attempt to do all things full speed ahead and attempt to find a way to use the least amount of time and energy to reach a desired purpose. Reluctantly, I must confess that I thought soaking beans, peas, and the like was a huge waste of time and for years I just rinsed my beans before cooking them.

My flippant, rushed attitude about the soaking procedure was a huge mistake. I am learning that patience is always rewarded and that there is a reason for the "madness" of waiting. Without soaking your beans and peas, digestive ills such as gas, heartburn, and reflux are a likely result. Upon soaking legumes in cold water, phytic acid and enzyme inhibitors are released producing a scum that rises to the top of the water. Once the scum is removed, you are much less vulnerable to bloating and digestive issues. Go now and enjoy your favorite 15-bean soup or a huge bowl of healthy black-eyed peas and homemade jalapeno cornbread!

Heirloom Black-eyed Peas

Refrigerator Dill Pickles

Yields 2 quarts

With as many babies as I have had, you know I know pickles! No, really. These truly are the best pickles, and they go great with Quarter Pound Turkey Burgers (p. 118) or the occasional bowl of Cantaloupe Ice Cream (p. 43).

Ingredients

1½ pounds fresh cucumbers	1 cup distilled white vinegar
2 onions, thinly sliced	½ cup sugar
8 sprigs of dill	4 tablespoons salt
1 teaspoon whole allspice	6 cloves garlic, smashed
3 cups water	1½ teaspoon dill seed

1. Slice cucumbers and onions into ¼ inch rounds. Divide the slices evenly among 2 quart-sized sterilized jars. Add 4 sprigs of dill and ½ teaspoon of whole allspice to each jar.

2. Combine water, vinegar, sugar, salt, garlic, and dill seed in a medium saucepan. Bring to a boil then lower to simmer and cook for 5 minutes.

3. Ladle hot liquid into jars, leaving one inch of headspace. Set jars aside and let cool completely. Place lids securely on jars and store in refrigerator. They should last for up to six weeks.

Heirloom Black-eyed Peas

Serves 8

Eating black-eyed peas at my grandfather's house has always been a family tradition for bringing in the New Year. Growing up in the South, we have such an abundance of black-eyed peas, crowder peas, and butter beans from our gardens that we can and freeze them for an entire year's use. It is a staple in the Southern home and pairs well with fish and venison as well as being a main dish on its own accompanied with Jalapeno Cornbread (p. 33).

HINT: Make sure the bell pepper does not overcook. It will lose its color and its al dente texture.

Ingredients

4 cups heirloom fresh black-eyed peas	1 tablespoon butter	2 tablespoons olive oil
4 cups water or chicken stock	1 tablespoon kosher salt	¼ Vidalia onion, diced
	½ red bell pepper, diced	

1. Place black-eyed peas, chicken stock, butter, and salt into large saucepan. Bring to a boil, and then lower to simmer.

2. Meanwhile sauté bell peppers in olive oil until al dente. When peas are done (about 30 minutes of simmering) pour into bowl and sprinkle bell peppers and raw onions on top. Serve.

• Peas have an abundance of nitrogen. Sometimes they are planted solely for their nitrogen content.

Herbs

When I think about herbs, my mind automatically thinks of the words beautiful, fragrant, and tasty, but herbs go much deeper than that. Throughout all of history people have used herbs medicinally as an antiseptic, antibiotic, or even as a relaxant. Herbs have many functions and can grow easily just about anywhere. Herbs can be grown indoors in pots and outdoors in the ground as a shrub or in a pot by the door. If nothing else tempts you to grow your own herbs, the mere fact that your food will begin to taste like a five-star restaurant with the simple use of fresh herbs. The one drawback is that you may never want to eat out again!

Herbs grown indoors need at least six hours of sunlight. I do not have windows in my kitchen, but I have large porches for containers, a designated spot between two sets of stairs right off the porch near the kitchen, and an herb garden for growing herbs.

I love to mix edible flowers in with my herbs as well as to plant herbs as shrubbery.

I have planted rosemary as a foundation plant and have layered other herbs such as lemongrass, basil, oregano, thyme, and sage intermixed with flowers for about two feet into the yard. I love to border with my beloved strawberries. These herbs are incredibly easy to grow and I adore the untamed look of all of them growing together.

This year I have planted an Italian Herb Pot and an old fountain with onions and parsley. Not only are they beautiful and functional, they make it easy for the small children to collect the herbs to go on my Quail Pizza! The Italian Herb Pot consists of basil, Italian parsley, marjoram, sage, rosemary and thyme.

The key to healthy herbs is to keep them moist. If you live in a dry climate, mist your herbs often. Herbs also love to be harvested often for optimal health and productivity of the plant. Don't forget to dry or freeze your herbs. Enjoy a fantastic culinary experience!

Herb Salad with Simple Vinaigrette

Serves 4-6

Herb salad is the epitome of freshness. It reminds me of those beautiful 75-degree days that we rarely see in Alabama. This light and refreshing salad would be perfect for a brunch.

Salad Ingredients

4 cups lettuce mix

¼ cup parsley leaves

¼ cup chives, cut into 1-inch pieces

¼ cup mint leaves

½ cup edible flowers

½ cup vinaigrette

Simple Vinaigrette Ingredients

3 tablespoons salad vinegar

6 tablespoons olive oil

½ teaspoon kosher salt

¼ teaspoon freshly ground pepper

1. In a small bowl, add vinegar. Slowly whisk oil into vinegar mixing constantly to form an emulsion. Add salt and pepper.

2. Combine lettuce, herbs and flowers in a medium sized bowl. Stir in about ¼ cup Simple Vinaigrette. Gently combine. Drizzle with extra vinaigrette as desired.

• All flowers in the rose family are edible as well as impatiens, pansies, marigolds, dandelions, and goldenrod.

Herb Frittata

Serves 4 - 6

This recipe reminds me of spring mornings and is one of the first recipes that I make when my herb garden begins to bloom. I would grow herbs just for this frittata!!

Ingredients

8 large eggs

2 teaspoons kosher salt

½ teaspoon freshly ground pepper

2 tablespoons fresh thyme, chopped

2 tablespoon sage leaves, chopped

½ cup Italian parsley leaves, chopped

½ cup fresh basil leaves, chopped

1 shallot, diced

1 cup mozzarella cheese, shredded

4 tablespoons butter

1. Place rack in oven close to the broiler and set broiler on high.

2. In a large bowl, blend eggs with salt and pepper until frothy.

3. Add thyme, sage, parsley, basil, shallots, and cheese to egg mixture and blend.

4. In an 8- to 10-inch sauté pan, heat butter until it begins to bubble. Add the egg mixture and cook over medium heat for 5 minutes or until it is set on the bottom and sides of pan. Transfer pan to the oven and broil for about 3 minutes or until the eggs are puffed and lightly browned. Sprinkle with parsley and serve.

Herb Balsamic Vinaigrette

Yields about 1½ cups

This vinaigrette is made with several of the most healthful ingredients known to man. It is especially great served over cabbage, fish, or turkey, and for dipping raw or cooked vegetables. Do not forget to drizzle over breads and pizza as well.

• Balsamic vinegar is filled with antioxidants and contains pepsin which improves the body's metabolism.

Ingredients

½ cup balsamic vinegar

2 tablespoons honey

1 teaspoon Dijon mustard

1 teaspoon salt

Freshly ground pepper to taste

2 teaspoons fresh basil, finely chopped

2 teaspoons fresh parsley, chopped

2 teaspoons fresh oregano, chopped

1 cup olive oil

1. Mix first 8 ingredients in a large bowl. Slowly pour olive oil into mixture while continuously whisking to ensure an emulsion.

Herb Frittata

Basil

Sweet basil, sometimes known as Saint Joseph's Wort, is typically found in Italian cuisine, but there are other varieties that are excellent as well including lemon, cinnamon, and Thai basil. Basil is also known as the "king of herbs" or as the "holy herb." Basil truly is a fascinating and healthy herb. It contains flavonoids, which protect cell structure and chromosomes from radiation and oxygen-based damage as well as being full of vitamins A and K.

Basil is incredibly easy to grow. It grows just about anywhere including the cracks between the bricks in my walkway. Of course, I do live in basil's favorite environment. Basil loves hot, dry environments. If you live in a cold environment, basil will grow well in a pot placed near a south-facing window. Let it dry out completely, then water it.

To promote more growth, pick the leaves often. Once the basil is allowed to flower, you can save the small black seeds and plant them the following year.

Basil Pesto

Yields about 2 cups

Basil pesto is incredibly versatile. I like to serve it over hot noodles, with eggplant parmesan, fried squash or over eggs.

HINT: Place a thin layer of olive oil over pesto and store pesto in refrigerator. It will keep it from browning.

HINT: If you are going to freeze, omit the cheese and add after the pesto has thawed. Because the cheese is omitted, the pesto will be a bit runny; it will thicken once you thaw and process with cheese. TO FREEZE line an ice cube tray with plastic wrap, and fill each pocket with pesto. Freeze and remove from tray and store in freezer bag. When ready to use, defrost and add cheese. Freeze for up to 3 months.

• Basil is used as an insect repellent for us and our gardens!

Ingredients

¼ cup pine nuts
3 cloves garlic
½ teaspoon kosher salt

½ teaspoon freshly ground black pepper
¾ cup olive oil

2½ cups basil leaves
1 cup Romano cheese

1. In a food processor fitted with the steel blade, place pine nuts, garlic, basil, Romano, salt and pepper. Slowly feed olive oil through feed tube of processor and process until pureed.

Preserving Summer

Oh, yes, you can do this. All you have to do is be prepared and have the right tools available and plenty of fresh fruits and vegetables. Almost anything can be preserved in some way, either, by canning, freezing or drying.

People think that canning or drying foods is scary and difficult, but just the opposite; it's healthy and easy. When you can, dry, and freeze the produce you have grown, you know absolutely everything that has gone into those vegetables and fruits. You are taking charge of your own health and food. Not only are you taking charge of your family's health and the food that they eat, you are working together as a family for a common good and enjoying relationships that will last for a lifetime, not to mention extra money from any surplus that you sell. Every year my family sells canned figs, mint jellies, and other preserves at an upscale arts-and-crafts show in our community. We sell a lot of different items, but the canned preserves are always the first to go and at a high price, too!

Canning

There are two main approaches to canning; the boiling water canning method and the pressure canning method. Fruits and tomatoes may be processed using the boiling water method found below, but the United States Department of Agriculture recommends that the pressure canner method is the only safe method for canning low acid foods such as vegetables, poultry and meats. If using the pressure canner method, always be sure to follow instructions in your manual. The steps will be the same as the boiling method of canning up until you place the jars into the canner.

Boiling Method

Tools

Large stockpot

Canning rack insert for stockpot

Ladle

Funnel

Tongs (with coated handles) for lifting jars

Glass canning jars

Magnetic lid lifter

Lids

Bands

Saucepan for sterilizing lids

Clean dish towels

These supplies can be bought at your local supermarket as a 9- or 12-piece canning kit.

Step 1

HINT: Always check the pH of your recipe before canning if using the boiling method. The pH needs to be 4.5 or lower to safely use the boiling method.

STERILIZE

• The sterilization option on your dishwasher will handle the sterilization process.

Organize and prepare before beginning. Always read your recipe carefully and thoroughly, and gather all of your equipment and ingredients. Make sure all equipment is in good condition with no broken or cracked jars or rusted bands. Always use new lids. Place glass jars in a large stockpot covered with water. Bring the water to a boil and continue to boil for 10 minutes. As you are ready to fill the jars, lift them out carefully with the jar lifter, emptying the water. Place these sterilized jars on a clean dish towel, butcher paper or paper towels.

Bring a small saucepan of water to a simmer and remove from heat. Drop the jar lids into the saucepan, cover the pan and let lids warm for at least 10 minutes. The lids should not be removed until the jars are ready to be sealed. A magnetic lid lifter makes it easier to remove the lids from the pan. The jars and lids are now sterilized.

Step 2

PREPARE RECIPE, SEAL, AND PROCESS

Prepare the recipe as directed. Ladle the mixture into the sterilized jars leaving a half-inch air space at the top. Remove all bubbles, wipe excess mixture from the threads of the jars, place sterilized lid on each jar using a magnetic lid lifter. Screw the bands onto the jars securely. Immediately, place the jars into the canning rack. Boil the jars in water 2-3 inches over the top of the jars. Keep the water at that level and boiling until you have reached the specified processing time. Times will vary depending on sizes of jars and ingredients. Let the jars cool in the canner for a few minutes and then remove. Place processed jars on a kitchen towel and allow cooling for 12-24 hours. These may be stored for up to one year or longer.

If you are preparing a recipe low in acid, you will need to use the **PRESSURE CANNING METHOD**. All of the steps of canning are the same until the water is placed inside the canner. If Pressure Canning, place 2 to 3 inches of water in the canner, then place the rack and jars inside, being careful not to allow the jars to touch each other or the sides of the canner. Snap the lid closed. Place canner over heat source set relatively high until a steady flow of steam can be seen coming form the vent pipe. Allow steam to escape for 10 minutes. Place the correct weight on the vent to pressurize the canner (the correct weight will be given in your canner instruction manual). Begin timing when the weight starts to wiggle or the gauge reads the correct pressure. Keep the heat as even as possible and when the time is up remove canner from heat. Allow the pressure to return to zero and release the steam. Open lid and direct steam away from you. Remove jars and place on a rack or kitchen towel and allow to slowly cool.

If lids do not "pop" down or you notice that the middle of the lid gives under pressure, place in the refrigerator and enjoy for a few months. These jars did not process properly.

Do not forget to label and date. Personalize your creations with labels, pieces of cloth and ribbons. You will love these as you begin to use them – they might even be given for gifts, or taken to parties. ENJOY!

Homemade Canned Tomatoes

I use canned tomatoes for a good portion of my recipes. In my opinion, tomatoes give flavor that no other vegetable can give. In the summer, it is like a factory in my kitchen as we can tomatoes day and night so as not to let even one of our precious tomatoes over-ripen. As a diversion, we prepare and snack on salsa while we continue our vigil of canning.

1. Drop tomatoes in boiling water for about 20 seconds. Remove from hot water. Remove skin from tomatoes by cutting off the stem end of tomato and squeezing from bottom.

2. Push down into a sterilized Mason jar. Add 2 teaspoons of lemon juice. Fasten lid tightly.

3. Submerge Mason jar in water. Bring to a boil and continue boiling for 40 minutes for pint-sized jars and 45 minutes for quart-sized jars. Once opened, keep refrigerated. They should last in refrigerator for a couple of weeks.

Granny's Garden Vegetable Soup

Granny's Garden Vegetable Soup

My grandmother was one of the best Southern cooks I have ever known and my dad is one of the best gardeners I know. The pair could make a mean soup—I could live on this soup forever!

HINT: Adding freshly squeezed lemon always brightens a dish!

Ingredients

3 tablespoons olive oil

2 celery stalks, chopped

1 large onion, chopped

1 clove garlic, crushed

2 pounds okra, sliced into ¼ inch thick rounds

8-10 tomatoes, peeled and crushed

¾ cup butter beans

4 ears of corn (1 cup), cut off the cob

1 tablespoon basil, chopped

1 tablespoon thyme, chopped

3 dashes of hot sauce

1 tablespoon salt

½ teaspoon pepper

1 lemon

1. In a large stockpot, heat olive oil over medium heat. Add celery, onions, and garlic and heat for about 1 minute stirring constantly.

2. Add okra, tomatoes, beans, corn, basil, thyme, hot sauce, salt, and pepper to the pot. Squeeze the lemon over soup. Add enough water to just cover the vegetables.

3. Bring mixture to a boil, and then reduce to simmer. Cover and let simmer for 1 hour.

4. Enjoy now with Jalapeno Cornbread (p. 33) or use pressure canner method to can this recipe. You will need 10 pounds of pressure for 1 hour and 25 minutes, and 1 inch of head space for this recipe. Adjust for altitude.

Fig Preserves

Yields 2 pints

Ingredients

1 pound fresh ripe figs

1 cup sugar

2 tablespoons lemon juice

1. Combine figs, sugar, and lemon juice together in a medium-sized saucepan and cook on low heat for 30 minutes uncovered.

2. Process 10 minutes using the boiling method as described on page 54.

Fresh Salsa

This salsa requires fresh, vine ripened vegetables to get the full flavor I enjoy so much. As soon as my vegetables are ripe, I bring them in and make this perfect sweet-and-spicy salsa!

HINT: Place a bowl upside down over the roasted vegetables for 5 minutes while allowing them to cool. It will make peeling them easier.

Ingredients

5 medium-sized tomatoes (½ pound)

2 jalapeno chilies

1 red bell pepper

1 lime, juiced

1 tablespoon olive oil

1 tablespoon cilantro

1 teaspoon salt

1. Preheat oven to 500 degrees. Core the tomatoes and halve lengthwise. Place the tomatoes cut-side down on a lined cookie sheet. Add the whole jalapeno and bell peppers on the cookie sheet and roast for 7-10 minutes, or until skin is charred. Turn peppers occasionally.

2. When cool, remove skin from vegetables plus the seeds from the peppers and place in food processor. Add remaining ingredients to a food processor.

3. Pulse food processor until almost smooth. Serve immediately or refrigerate for up to one week. If canning and using pressure canning method, process for 1 hour and 25 minutes and leave a ½-inch of head space for this recipe. If you would rather have pint-sized jars you will need 10 pounds of pressure for 55 minutes and a ½-inch of head space. If using the boiling method, lower the pH at least to 4.5 by adding 2 tablespoon of lemon juice to each pint-sized jar. Adjust for altitude.

Salsa Verde
(the tomatillo sauce)

• Pick tomatillos at the peak of freshness, when yellow, for best flavor.

Ingredients

10 medium-sized tomatillos (2 ounces), husk removed, cored, and cut in half lengthwise

1 jalapeno chili

1 Vidalia or yellow onion, quartered

2 cloves garlic

3 tablespoons fresh cilantro

1 lime, juiced

Salt and pepper to taste

1. Preheat oven to 500 degrees. Place tomatillos cut-side up along with the whole jalapenos on a baking sheet and roast for 7-10 minutes or until black spots appear on tomatillos. Turn baking sheet halfway through roasting process.

2. When cool, remove as much skin as possible from vegetables along with the jalapeno chili seeds and stem. Place in food processor. Add onions, garlic, cilantro, and lime juice and purée to the consistency of your liking. Salt and add pepper to taste.

3. Serve immediately or refrigerate for up to one week. If canning, and using pressure canning method, process for 1 hour and 25 minutes and leave a ½-inch of head space for this recipe. If you would rather have pint-sized jars you will need 10 pounds of pressure for 55 minutes and a ½-inch of head space. If using the boiling method, lower the pH at least to 4.5 by adding 2 tablespoon of lemon juice to each pint-sized jar. Adjust for altitude.

Freezing

Freezing is a great way to preserve your harvest. This is my favorite way to preserve meat as well as many vegetables and fruits.

Freezing meat is a must for those of you buying whole cows or those who hunt large game. Meat can be canned and dried, but freezing saves room and allows for more options in cooking. After allowing freshly harvested meat such as poultry, wild game, or recently butchered beef to age, wrap it in airtight, moisture-proof containers. Of course, there are vacuum sealers are excellent for freezing your meats and produce. There are freezer jars and plastic containers, but my favorite is freezer paper. It saves room and is easy to label. There are great instructions that come with the freezer paper. I like to double-wrap the meat to ensure freshness. Always thaw your meat in the refrigerator.

When freezing fruit, I have found it best not to wash the fruit, but to brush any visible debris from the fruit instead. Washing the fruit tends to make it mushy upon thawing. Take your harvest and freeze individually on a cookie sheet. Once frozen, grab a freezer bag and fill it with your frozen fruit and place back into freezer. It is as easy as that!

When freezing fresh vegetables, always clean them, check them carefully for dirt or other debris. Once they are clean, the next step is blanching. **BLANCHING** consists of boiling the raw vegetables for 2-3 minutes and then stopping the blanching process by cooling. Cooling is accomplished by placing the vegetables immediately into cool-to-cold water. This completely stops the cooking process and the vegetables are then ready to be placed in freezer bags or containers and frozen until you are ready to enjoy them.

Drying

Drying is perhaps the oldest method of preserving. It dates back to the days of our ancient ancestors and Native Americans. They preserved their harvests long before canners, pressure cookers, and freezers were invented. They sun-dried their fruits and vegetables, but I prefer using the oven. I do not have to deal with insects that way! It is easy to dry fruits, vegetables, herbs, and even chili peppers. You more than likely already have all that is needed to pursue preservation by this method.

DRYING BEANS AND PEPPERS

1. Wash your harvest and string your beans, peppers, and herbs together with a needle and heavy-duty thread or fishing line, making a knot around each bean.

2. Repeat until the thread is full and then simply hang these beans for several months in a dry place.

DRYING FRUITS AND VEGETABLES

One of my favorite methods of drying is to use the oven (or a dehydrator). My children especially love preserving their harvest by this method. They love making dried peaches, apples, figs, and berries. I love for them to preserve by using the drying method as they eat these delicious fruits and berries as snacks rather than snacks chock full of sugars and artificial ingredients that seem to have made their way into our diets via the grocery store. Preserving really offers us a much healthier way of living our lives If using a dehydrator, follow the instructions in your manual.

DRYING USING OVEN

1. Set the oven to the lowest possible setting.

2. Slice your fruits and vegetables into thin pieces and place on a cookie sheet.

3. Cook overnight or until all moisture is removed.

- If you do not like leaving the oven on all night, drying can be done throughout several days. Just remove the cookie sheet from the oven and begin drying them the next day in the same manner.

4. Store your dried goods packed in freezer bags or in food-saver packets. Freeze them for up to one year.

And, let's not forget jerky. My men love their jerky. After they have prepared the finer venison for the freezer, they use the less desired meat for jerky. The result is another wonderfully healthy snack loaded with protein.

1. Heat the oven to 200 degrees.

2. Thinly slice meat and season as you desire.

3. Place meat about ½-inch apart on a cookie sheet.

3. Bake for six hours.

Drying Figs

HINT: Drying figs in a food dehydrator will work equally well. Follow the manufacturer's instructions.

1. Set your oven on the lowest setting. It is probably around 135 degrees.

2. Remove stems, cut figs in half, and lay them flesh-side up on the cookie sheet turning occasionally for 24 hours or until the outsides are leathery and there are no juices when you put pressure on the figs. Keep the oven door slightly open so that the figs dry instead of cook. You can do this in 12-hour cycles by turning the oven off during the night if you choose.

3. Store figs in an air-tight container for several months. Figs will last in the freezer for up to 24 months.

Composing

Composting improves the soil and reduces waste, not to mention saves money on fertilizer. The only requirement for composting is to have a special receptacle to discard certain types of kitchen wastes, such as fruit and vegetable peels, as well as dead leaves and grasses or remnants from a spent garden. Composting is great for our family because trash builds up quickly with a house of nine members. Receptacles can range from a container on the kitchen counter filled to a large, outdoor professional composting bin. Composting can be accomplished through several inexpensive methods such as worm composting, composting tumblers that you purchase at your local garden store, or a backyard composting structure. Compost degrades naturally, creating healthy fertilizer and mulching material for your lawn or garden.

To begin composting simply place a layer of about six inches of green ingredients (kitchen waste, hair, garden waste, grass clippings) in the bottom of your receptacle, soak with water, then layer about two inches of brown ingredients (wood chips, straw, dry leaves, sawdust), then continue to layer and turn periodically. To speed the process of composting you can add an activator which can also be purchased at your garden store. As your gardens grow, the need for more compost is important in putting nourishment back into the ground. Green material is high in nitrogen and the brown material is high in carbon.

The boys built a double bin this year. They use one side for composting and the other for dressing deer. Multiple deer carcasses can become mulch within a few months and will add incredible minerals, nutrients, and beneficial bacteria to the soil.

Beyond The GARDEN

- Foraging Wild Fruits, Herbs, and Greens
- Beekeeping
- Poultry and Eggs

Foraging Wild Fruits, Herbs, and Greens

Foraging or "living off the land" as my kids like to call it, is one of our family's favorite hobbies, or I should say adventures. There is something so special about being out in God's creation, picking the plants and herbs He provides for us, and making meals from what we harvest. One of my favorite things is being able to snack on the things I have just picked. There is nothing more organic than that!

All of us have a natural foraging instinct that cannot be quenched in a grocery store shopping experience. Even though many health markets are offering wild herbs and vegetables such as dandelion greens and wood sorrel, there is nothing like being out in the fresh air and picking your own. We love to go on hikes each spring on a berry expedition and competition. Whoever fills their bags the fastest with wild berries gets the first piece of the homemade pie made from the berries.

When I was younger, my dad would take me to visit my cousins who lived way out in the country. They had a great big crab apple tree next to a trampoline, and I thought it was the greatest thing that we could just pick a snack off the tree and lie down on the trampoline and eat to our hearts' desires. Every child, or adult for that matter, needs this kind of rest and recreation in the wild open world. Seeing my children picking crab apples off the tree or eating ripe persimmons and muscadines reminds me of those sweet childhood memories.

Some of our very favorite plants to forage are sassafras and purslane. There is an overgrown road behind our house that grows sassafras trees profusely. Sassafras was one of the largest exports from America second only to tobacco in the 1600s. We use it as a thickener in soups and gumbo as well as for tea. The sassafras adds a slight licorice taste to the tea and gives root beer its licorice flavor.

Our farm, in Central Alabama is full of purslane. It is a leafy vegetable of which stems, leaves, and flower buds are edible. Purslane has the highest amount of Omega-3 fatty acids of any vegetable. We use purslane in salads as well as sauté them for a bed underneath fish in that their tangy flavor enhances in much the same way as lemon or lime.

The nutritional values of wild herbs and fruits are amazingly high compared to their domestic counterparts. Wild berries such as blackberries, huckleberries, elderberries, and dewberries contain more of the powerful antioxidant anthocyanin as well as taste tangier and sweeter than domestic berries. Anthocyanin is believed to protect against brain aging and to promote vision health. Fruits and berries are nature's candy. A crab apple has twice the fiber as regular apples. These are just a few examples of the extraordinary benefits of eating wild.

Our ancestors "lived off the land" whether they hunted, raised, or gathered their food. There is a satisfaction and a great reward in harvesting wild proteins, herbs, vegetables, and fruits for your self. Not only do you feel accomplished, but also you save money, eat healthier, and enjoy the taste of the freshest foods available. We enjoy the process of surviving off the land and making use of the great bounty found in nature. We hope that you and your family will enjoy it as much as we do.

Note:

• The extremely invasive Kudzu vine has been consumed during famines in Japan and saved many lives. Not only is Kudzu higher in calories than most herbs, it increases circulation to reduce pain and stiffness, and has been used as a beta blocker for racing pulse induced by stress.

Wild Turkey, Dandelion Greens, Wood Sorrel, and Greenbrier with Balsamic Herb Vinaigrette

Serves 4

Dandelions have been attributed to curing liver disease, preventing and curing high blood pressure, preventing various forms of cancer and assisting in weight reduction. On top of being delicious, this meal is healthy. Most folks could walk right into their backyards and have a nutritious meal on the table within minutes!

• This is truly a seasonal dish. All the ingredients are ripe for harvest simultaneously in the spring.

• Dandelions have been used in anti-plaque preparations by dental researchers.

• Greenbrier is available in most supermarkets. If you cannot find it, just add more dandelion greens. Greenbrier is in the smilax family, which is most notable for providing sarsaparilla found in root beer, and it is rumored that the smilax steroid treats dementia and Alzheimer's disease.

Ingredients

3 cups dandelion greens

⅓ cup greenbrier

⅓ cup wood sorrel

⅓ cup green onions

¼ cup mulberries

¼ cup strawberries

¼ cup serviceberries

1 cup Herb Balsamic Vinaigrette (p. 50)

1 pound turkey breast, 1-inch slices

2 tablespoons olive oil

1 tablespoon kosher salt

1 teaspoon freshly ground pepper

1. In a large bowl, place ½ cup of the Herb Balsamic Vinaigrette. Gently mix dandelion greens, greenbrier, wood sorrel, onions, mulberries, strawberries, and serviceberries with the vinaigrette and divide greens among four plates.

2. Pound each turkey slice to about ⅛ inch thick and cut into bite sized pieces.

3. In a medium-sized bowl, mix olive oil, salt, pepper and turkey pieces together.

4. Heat cast iron skillet to almost smoking and cook turkey pieces in batches for 2 minutes on each side. Be sure not to crowd the pan so that your meat browns and does not steam.

5. Divide turkey pieces among the four salad plates. Drizzle a little Herb Balsamic Vinaigrette over the salad as desired. Serve with your favorite Crusty Bread.

Wild Turkey, Dandelion Greens, Wood Sorrel, and Greenbrier with Balsamic Herb Vinaigrette

Wild Blueberry Pie

Serves 8

One of my favorite times of the year is late spring when all of our wild blueberries are ripe. Our family tradition is to see who can pick the most berries. Mary, my 8- year-old, won this year, but I think it is due to her self-control. Everyone else was digging into their stash and she saved every one of hers. We come home, announce winners, make this awesome Wild Blueberry Pie and give the first slice to the winner. I hope this tradition lasts through the generations.

• You can substitute domestic cultivated berries in the pie if wild berries are not in season.

• Brushing the top lattice with heavy cream or an egg and sprinkling raw sugar on the tops of the lattice crust gives it a prettier appearance as well as a nice crunch.

Ingredients

2 homemade pie crusts
5½ cups blueberries
⅓ cup brown sugar

⅓ cup granulated sugar, plus 2 tablespoons for sprinkling
1 teaspoon cinnamon

¼ cup flour, plus 2 tablespoons for sprinkling
1 large egg, beaten (optional)
1 tablespoon heavy cream (optional)

1. Preheat oven to 375 degrees.

2. In a large bowl combine berries, brown sugar, granulated sugar, cinnamon and flour. Stir gently.

3. Sprinkle 2 tablespoons of flour and 2 tablespoons of granulated sugar on the bottom of chilled crust. Place bottom crust into a deep-dish pie plate. Pour filling into the crust, follow lattice crust instructions for second pie crust (p. 25) and bake for one hour or until blueberries are bubbly and crust is golden. Serve with ice cream or homemade whipped cream.

Sassafras Tea

Makes 1 Gallon

The sassafras tree has been historically a very important tree. At one point in the 1600s it was one of the largest exports from America, second only to tobacco. The Creoles and the Cajuns learned from the Indians the thickening qualities of sassafras leaves and it soon became part of their cuisines. The roots of the tree became the key ingredient in the original root beer or could be made into a delightful tea.

Our family loves sassafras tea; there is nothing quite like it. The only way I can describe the taste is something like a fruity licorice drink. If you want to make this classic tea, then follow the simple recipe below.

1. If you have your own property, or permission of a landowner, walk along the sides of the roads and look for a 3- to 5-foot sassafras sapling.

2. Once located, slowly ease the tree up by pulling as low down on the tree as you can, trying to recover as much of the tap root as possible (You might have to loosen the soil with a shovel).

3. Take a pair of garden sheers and cut the root away from the trunk. Keep the top of the tree if you plan on making filé. Wash the roots well.

4. Weigh out two ounces of root and cut into 1-inch pieces.

5. Place the root pieces straight into a pot of water and bring to a simmer. Let simmer for 5 minutes then allow to cool for another 10 minutes for maximum flavor.

6. Meanwhile, measure 1½ cups of sugar and place in a gallon pitcher.

7. Set a cheesecloth over the pitcher and fasten it with a rubber band.

8. Pour in the tea and stir to dissolve sugar.

9. Chill and serve over ice. Enjoy!

Now you are left with a bunch of sassafras tree tops. In Louisiana the Creoles and the Cajuns make a killer gumbo using powdered sassafras leaves they call filé powder. Here is how to make this Southern thickener.

Filé Powder

1. Bundle several sassafras branches and hang in your attic, basement, or garage. It is best to keep it in a dark, dry environment.

2. When dry, remove leaves and place in a food processor.

3. Chop until a very fine powder, about 2 minutes.

4. Sift the filé powder to rid it of stem bases.

5. Place in an airtight container and store in a cool, dark place. It should keep for one year.

You can use filé powder in gumbo and soups in place of roux or okra. Just slowly add until you have desired consistency. The flavor of the filé itself is light but has a slight earthy taste that adds richness and body to the dish. It can also be used as a final garnish. Bon appétite!

Beekeeping

Solomon, the wisest man in the world, said these words to his son, "My son, eat thou honey, because it is good, and the honeycomb is sweet to thy taste." Bees have been a huge part of history and culture from the beginning of time. One of the earliest noted references to beekeeping was around 3,000 BC whereby a beekeeper near the Nile River begged for someone to send his donkeys to transport his hives before the flood demolished them. Honey has been and is still today a treasured commodity associated with health and prosperity. In the book of Exodus, the Israelites were promised to dwell in a land "flowing with milk and honey." There is no greater sweetener than honey in the world and the health benefits are amazing.

I must admit that upon our bees' arrival, I was a little apprehensive. It did not take me very long to learn to love them though. They gently let you know when you are being intrusive by racing toward you and slamming into your forehead. I can't lie; my stomach still drops and I get a rush of adrenaline when this warning from my bees occurs. The kids love tending to the hives as if they are our pets, and kind of they are. They work very hard for us collecting pollen and making loads of honey. I see appreciation from the kids as they nurture and protect these wonderful honeybees.

It seems that the medicinal, culinary, and household uses of honey and wax are endless. Honey needs little digestion, giving a quick energy boost without the crash of white sugar and other carbohydrates. Honey is known as an antiseptic, sleep aid, immunity booster, anti-inflammatory, circulation increaser, in addition to being the main component in a tincture to stave off colds or treat a sore throat. Bee stings have been known to manage pain in arthritic patients and a tablespoon of local honey taken once a day will eradicate allergy symptoms.

Bees are a gardener's best friend in that 80% of all pollination that takes place is done by bees. Gardener's have better productivity of fruits, flowers, and vegetables. Wildlife also benefits from greater amounts of clover fields, fruit trees, fruit-bearing bushes, and wild herbs and plants.

Beeswax contributes to many households in the form of beautiful and natural furniture wax, water repellent, and candles.

I am ever so thankful to the Colonists for importing bees to the United States in the 1600s. Our gardens have better yield, our food has better flavor, our bodies are healthier, and our skin ages less rapidly when using products with honey in them. The benefits of beekeeping far outweigh the time involved. It only takes about one hour a week and one day twice a year to harvest the honey. Your yield will be well worth it as well as the benefit to the community. If you do not have time to devote to beekeeping, please support your local beekeepers.

If you are interested in beekeeping contact your local beekeepers association. There are many beekeeping supply companies that can help you get started as well. They will supply you with protective clothing, hives, tools, and bees. Bees are like caring for any other special pet. They need protection from the elements, water, food, and lots of love and appreciation!

Facts:

- You are more likely to get stung on a cloudy, windy, or rainy day.
- Almost all commercial bees are treated with various chemicals and medications.
- One worker bee will visit 100 flowers per collection trip but only make a one-half tablespoon of honey in a lifetime.
- It takes two million flowers pollinated to produce one jar of honey.
- Honey helps burn fat while you sleep.
- One tablespoon of honey taken four times a day relieves pain of stomach ulcers.
- Honey will store indefinitely. Honey has been found in Egyptian tombs dating back 3,300 years ago and in great condition.

Cinnamon Pear Buns with Honey Bourbon Sauce

Serves 4

Cinnamon Pear Buns are a cross between cinnamon buns and homemade apple pie. These two American comfort foods combined together are a delight at any breakfast table or even for dessert. Because there is no yeast in this recipe, they are quick and easy to make. I also love the fact that I get pears, oranges, and honey all in one bite. If you have leftover Honey Bourbon Sauce, it makes for a great ice cream topping!

Ingredients

2 cups all-purpose flour
4 teaspoons baking powder
½ teaspoon salt
¼ cup shortening
¾ cup buttermilk
2 pears, diced
½ cup sugar
1 teaspoon cinnamon
½ stick melted butter (4 tablespoons)

Honey Bourbon Sauce

1½ cups honey
2 tablespoons cornstarch
Juice of one orange
3 tablespoons bourbon
⅛ teaspoon salt

1. Pre-heat oven to 400 degrees.

2. In a large bowl, mix flour, baking powder, and salt.

3. Work the shortening into the dry ingredients quickly with your hands then add the buttermilk without overworking.

4. In a small bow, mix sugar and cinnamon.

5. Roll dough out to ¼-inch thick rectangle. Cover the rectangle with the diced pears leaving a ½-inch border around the edges and sprinkle the cinnamon sugar mixture on top of the pears. Beginning at the end farthest from you(this should be the long end of the roll), roll the rectangle towards you then cut the log into eight 1-inch slices.

6. Butter a baking dish and place the cinnamon rolls into the dish. Distribute the melted butter equally over the top of the buns and place them in the oven for 20-25 minutes or until golden brown.

7. Meanwhile, prepare the bourbon sauce by combining the honey, cornstarch, juice of one orange, bourbon, and salt in a small saucepan. Heat sauce over medium heat and reduce by about a third. This should take 10 minutes. Stir mixture often.

8. Remove the buns from the oven and serve with warm sauce.

Cinnamon Pear Buns with Honey Bourbon Sauce

Baked Peaches with Honey and Almonds

Honey Butter Sauce

Yields about ¾ cup

This sauce is great with waffles, pancakes, pound cakes, biscuits, and even over ice cream!

Ingredients

¼ cup butter, melted

¼ cup honey

¼ cup orange juice

½ teaspoon vanilla

1. In a medium-sized bowl, mix melted butter, honey, orange juice, and vanilla until well blended and smooth.

Baked Peaches with Honey and Almonds

Serves 8

Peaches are the epitome of summer in the south. About twenty miles north of our home is the peach capital of Alabama. There are several local peach farms that sell these juicy ripe peaches to peach markets located right by US I-65 in between Montgomery and Birmingham. Travelers must stop by and try their fabulously perfected peach ice cream. I love to devour peaches right off the tree from our yard, but as a special easy treat for the family, I love to make this recipe. The crunch and flavor of the almonds play perfectly with this decadent fruit!

• Peaches are rich in vitamin A, beta-carotene as well as potassium, fluoride, and iron. Peaches actually prevent tooth decay.

Ingredients

4 tablespoons butter

4 peaches halved, cored, and skinned

8 tablespoons skinned almonds

8 tablespoons honey

1. Preheat oven to 350 degrees. Place butter in bottom of casserole and melt butter.

2. Place peaches core-side up in baking dish.

3. In a small bowl, combine almonds and honey. Divide the honey mixture among the peaches. Bake in oven for 25 minutes or until peaches pierce easily with a knife. Serve with ice cream or whipped cream.

Melon Salad with Honey Poppy Seed Dressing

Melon Salad with Honey Poppy Seed Dressing

Serves 6

This recipe tastes like summer in a bowl! I love walking in the garden and seeing beautiful melons ripe for the picking. Freshly harvested honey with poppy seeds are a perfect and bright accompaniment that does not distract from the sweetness of the melons.

Ingredients

2 cups honeydew melon

2 cups muskmelon (cantaloupe)

2 cups watermelon

1 tablespoon mint, chopped

Honey Poppy Seed Dressing Ingredients

1½ cup olive oil

½ cup honey

⅓ cup salad vinegar

2 tablespoons Dijon mustard

2 tablespoons poppy seed

½ teaspoon salt

1. Cut melons in half. Scoop out seeds with spoon and discard.

2. With a melon ball scooper or mini ice cream scooper, scoop 1-inch balls and place in large bowl. Remove seeds from watermelon as you scoop.

3. In a food processor, mix all of the dressing ingredients until thick and emulsified. Stir in mint.

4. Pour one-quarter of the dressing over the fruit and coat the melons thoroughly. Store the remaining dressing in the refrigerator for up to two weeks.

Poultry and Eggs

Fun, beautiful, and perfect! That is how I feel about chickens. They are extremely smart and have very distinct, wonderful (at least most of the time) personalities. We have been raising chickens for over a decade and I never tire of watching them and getting to know each of them. Ever since the chicks' arrival our family has laughed chasing them around the yard, watching them strut, and listening to the roosters, which we did not know we had, show their dominance. They have produced the best eggs I have ever eaten and been a friend and entertainment for my 6-year-old daughter.

Scott and the kids had been talking for some time about raising chickens, but I really did not take them too seriously. They are always dreaming and planning something. One morning I woke up to banging and saw noises. They boys were creating a chicken tractor for the new baby chicks! Sure enough the post office called and said that I needed to pick up a box that was making a lot of noise. That was the beginning of our chicken adventure!

I certainly did not know what to do with these adorable baby chicks, but Scott and the kids had done the research. We set up a heating lamp in a large cage filled with hay and supplied them with water and food on our front porch. It was our own homemade brooder. At the end of the day the entire family went to bed with a feeling of accomplishment and the excitement of a new adventure, except me. I lay awake worrying that the chicks would be too hot or too cold, or the heating lamp would burn them somehow. I was already forming a motherly instinct toward them!

The chickens grew like children, that is like weeds! Five months passed and we got our first gorgeous light blue egg from our Ameraucana. They continued to lay eggs until winter when we noticed that we were only getting approximately one egg a week. The days were shorter and the chickens began molting. To continue to lay eggs, they would need a light in the chicken house. Chickens need fourteen hours of daylight to lay eggs on a consistent basis.

In that our family is fairly large, we needed more eggs than what our six hens were providing. We bought 12 more chicks and worked up to 50! They have been great for our garden as they search for insects. We do have to keep an eye on them or they will eat our produce. They love figs! Scott and the boys built a great little chicken coop and the boys all take turns tending to them. We still continue to use the chicken tractor for new chicks that are ready to roam, but not ready to be with the adult chickens. If the chicks are introduced to the adult hens too early, the hens will peck the poor chicks to death.

Raising chickens has been one of the most rewarding and beneficial decisions our family has made. Chickens supply us with one of the most versatile forms of protein on a self-sustaining farm, whether you raise the birds just for the eggs, or both the meat and eggs. Nothing goes into the chickens that you do not give them. There are no antibiotics, genetically modified organisms, or growth hormones in them. They are easy to care for and the harvest is no less than fabulous!

Because our chickens are fed scraps from the table and are given freedom to run around in the yard, they are healthier birds, therefore giving us healthier meat and eggs. Both the meat and eggs are higher in Omega-3 fatty acid, contain less cholesterol and saturated fat and more vitamins and folic acid than those of caged birds. The yolks of the eggs are richer in color and the meat from the old laying hens and roosters is more succulent and flavorful.

Some of you will decide never to dine on your beloved chickens, but if you ever have the chance to eat a meal prepared with an old rooster or laying hen, your taste buds will be enlightened and you will forever crave this heavenly delight! Roosters and aging hens need quite different treatment than your average fryer or broiler. As these chickens roam free and scratch for insects, they gain muscle and connective tissue, which produces incredible body in stews, dumplings, and broth because it melts into collagen as you braise it. The flavor of the broth and the chicken is exceptional and cannot be matched.

There are three major components to achieve tender domestic poultry.

1. Domestic laying hens or roosters must be refrigerated or aged for at least three days. (I age it for five days and keep it on a rack not allowing it to sit in any blood).

2. Braise it on low heat for at least three to five hours.

3. After braising, allow it to rest in the refrigerator overnight if time permits.

Truly, there is no more rewarding hobby than that of raising chickens. They are fun, encourage family relationships, produce great tasting eggs, and nourish the soul as well as the body, not to mention save on car fuel. You do not even have to leave your house to have the best meal you have ever had! Delicious!

Side notes:

- Our most consistent laying hens are Buff Orpingtons, Rhode Island Reds, Dominiques, and Ameraucanas. These hens lay large eggs and the Ameraucanas will give you a beautiful light blue/green egg.
- A chicken tractor is a moveable, low-to-the-ground chicken coop. As you move the chicken tractor, the chickens fertilize the ground as well as dine on nutritious grass and insects.

Tips:

- Feed your chickens from the table and give them lots of love and you will have happy chickens that lay "golden eggs!"
- Avoid washing eggs to protect the bloom. The bloom is the protective coating on the outside of the shell. If you must wash them, eat them within a few days in that they will not last as long as those that have not been washed. Some people recommend putting hand sanitizer on the outside to kill any bacteria right before cracking the egg.
- If you notice your eggshells are soft, bake eggshells in a 350-degree oven for 5 minutes, crush, and feed them to your chickens. This will give them extra calcium in their diets.

Rooster and Buttermilk Dumplings

Serves 8-10

One of my "foodie" friends, Tim Martin, shared his "Chicken and Dunklins" recipe with me in which I adapted to work with Roosters and old laying hens. The dumplings are so good that his son at the age of three emptied his first bowl of dumplings and cried, "More Dunklins Daddy!" Hence the name of his recipe!

- If you are using an organic chicken as opposed to a rooster or old hen, you may only need to simmer chicken for one hour.

- To reheat dumplings, place dumplings into a microwavable bowl and sprinkle a little water over the dumplings and microwave until hot. Stop every minute or so and stir as gently as possible.

Stock Ingredients

1 whole rooster, laying hen, or organic chicken
4 quarts (1 gallon) water
3 stalks celery, chopped
2 carrots
1 Vidalia or yellow onion, chopped
5 sprigs parsley

5 sprigs rosemary
3 whole garlic cloves
1 stick unsalted butter
1 tablespoon Kosher salt
½ tablespoon pepper

Dumplings

3 cups self-rising flour
½ cup shortening

2 teaspoons Kosher salt
½ cup buttermilk, plus more if dough is too dry

TIM'S HINT: If it's too dry, add a little buttermilk; too wet, dust with flour and continue to knead. It's OK to overwork dumpling dough.

1. Bring chicken, water, celery, carrots, onion, parsley, rosemary, and garlic to a boil, reduce heat and simmer uncovered for at least 3 hours or until the chicken falls off the bones. Make sure to skim the foam as needed.

2. Meanwhile, prepare the dumplings. In a large mixing bowl, combine flour and salt. Cut shortening into flour until fully incorporated. Add buttermilk slowly into the flour a little at the time. When the dough is easily formed into a ball, knead the dough.

3. Roll out the dough to a thickness of ¹⁄₁₆ of an inch or even thinner. Pinch or cut into 1 inch squares (I use a pizza cutter for this). Set aside.

4. When chicken is falling off the bone, remove the pieces to a plate. Strain the broth discarding vegetables and herbs.

5. Add broth back to the pot and add butter, salt and pepper. Bring to a boil and lower to a simmer. Pull all the meat from the chicken and shred. Return chicken to the broth.

6. Add the dumplings to the broth and bring to a hard boil. Allow them to boil about 2 minutes and turn off the heat. Stir gently with a wooden spoon every few minutes for the next 30 minutes. This step releases the starch in the dumplings, promotes creaminess, and intensifies the buttery flavors!

Rooster and Buttermilk Dumplings

Chicken and Mushrooms Over Cheesy Grits

Chicken and Mushrooms
Over Cheesy Grits

Serves 4

Comfort. That is what this meal represents. The garlic and tender chicken mixed with creamy, salty, cheesy grits and a gravy-like sauce with mushrooms...comfort...scrumptious...amazing!

HINT: Use any mushrooms available, but for best flavor use a variety of mushrooms. Just remember to keep the total amount of mushrooms the same as the recipe.

Ingredients

4 chicken thighs, skin removed and de-boned
½ teaspoon kosher salt
¼ teaspoon freshly ground pepper
¼ cup all-purpose flour
1 tablespoon olive oil
2 large onions, cut into 1-inch pieces
3 garlic cloves, minced

2 large carrots, cut into 1-inch pieces
8 ounces of Baby Bella mushrooms, halved
4 ounces button mushrooms, halved
4 ounces Shitake mushrooms, stemmed and sliced
1 tablespoon rosemary, chopped
1½ cups chicken broth

1. In a shallow dish, combine flour, salt, and pepper and coat the chicken in mixture. Reserve 1 tablespoon leftover flour. Place the oil in a large pot and heat over medium-high heat. When oil is shimmering, add the chicken and cook for 5-7 minutes or until brown on all sides. Remove to a plate.

2. Reduce the heat to medium, stir the onions into the pot, and cook for 2 minutes. Add garlic and cook for 30 seconds. Whisk in the reserved 1 tablespoon of flour and cook for 1 minute. Stir in chicken broth, carrots, mushrooms, and rosemary and place the chicken into the vegetables and bring to a boil. Partly cover and simmer over medium-low heat for 25-30 minutes, or until the chicken is no longer pink in the middle and the vegetables are tender. Plate warm, atop a scoop of cheese grits.

Cheesy Grits

Serves 4

• Do not add cheese until right before serving. The cheese will separate and become grainy.

Ingredients

5 cups water or chicken stock
1 cup grits, preferably stone-ground grits
3 tablespoons butter

½ teaspoon salt
½ teaspoon pepper
½ cup Parmesan-Reggiano

1. Add grits, butter, salt, and pepper to the water or stock. Bring to a boil stirring constantly, and then reduce to simmer for about 30 minutes, stirring occasionally.

2. Just before serving, add the Parmesan and stir until melted.

Chicken Farmer's Style

Chicken Farmer's Style

Serves 4

This dish really is one of my favorite preparations of old chickens. This is one of the first recipes I created from my studying historic French techniques for cooking old game hens. I have updated some of the ingredients but the technique remains the same.

• This recipe is great using pheasant.

Brine Ingredients

1 cup kosher salt

½ cup brown sugar

1 tablespoon peppercorns

2 scallions, chopped

2 cloves of garlic

¼ teaspoon allspice

1 quart chicken stock

2 quarts water

Ingredients

1 chicken, quartered and rinsed

Freshly ground black pepper

12 slices pancetta

2 tablespoons butter

2 tablespoons extra virgin olive oil

4 large carrots, cut into 1 inch lengths

3 cloves garlic, thinly sliced

1 onion, diced to ¼ inch

3 bay leaves

3 sprigs rosemary

3 stalk celery

1 cup dry white wine

1 pound whole Homemade Canned Tomatoes

Or 15 oz. canned tomatoes

¼ cup Italian parsley, finely chopped

1. Combine kosher salt, brown sugar, peppercorns, scallions, garlic, and allspice in a saucepan. Add chicken stock and bring to a boil, stirring to dissolve the salt and sugar. Remove from heat and allow to cool.

2. Combine the cooled mixture with water in a large pot big enough to hold the chicken and stir well. Add quartered chicken and refrigerate overnight.

3. Remove chicken from brine and pat dry with towels. Season with pepper.

4. Wrap each piece of quartered chicken in a slice of pancetta and secure with a toothpick. In skillet heat olive oil and butter over high heat. Add chicken and brown for about 10 minutes on each side. Do not crowd or they will not brown. Transfer to plate.

5. Add carrots, garlic, onion, bay leaves, rosemary, and celery to pan and cook about 5 minutes. Add the wine and tomatoes. Crush the tomatoes as you place them in the pot. Add chicken and reduce heat to simmer. Cook uncovered for about 30 minutes or until chicken is no longer pink. Transfer chicken to a serving platter.

6. Adjust seasoning. Add parsley. Pour sauce over meat. Serve with Garlic Mashed Potatoes (p. 35).

Healthy Chicken Soup

Serves 4

I can't help but feel warm and fuzzy every time my mom serves me chicken soup. I think she was a firm believer that chicken soup had medicinal properties. Who can argue with that?

- Chinese 5 spice, a blend of star anise, clover, fennel seed, cinnamon and Sichuan pepper, can be eliminated from this recipe, but I personally think it adds a special touch to the dish.

Ingredients

2 tablespoons olive oil

2 Vidalia onions, chopped

1 clove garlic, minced

4 cups celery, chopped

3 cups carrots, chopped

¾ cup Italian parsley, chopped and divided

2 tablespoons rosemary, chopped

¼ teaspoon Chinese 5 spice

4 pounds and 4 cups chicken meat, shredded

1 quart chicken stock

1 tablespoon kosher salt

½ teaspoon freshly ground pepper

1. In a large crock heat olive oil until simmering. Add onions and sauté until onions are translucent. Add garlic and sauté for 30 seconds more.

2. Add celery, carrots, ½ cup parsley, rosemary, Chinese 5 Spice, salt and pepper, chicken, and stock. Stir ingredients well.

3. Bring mixture to a boil then reduce heat and let simmer for 1 hour stirring occasionally. Ladle into bowls and serve with remaining parsley.

Homemade Chicken Stock

- Old hens and roosters have always been preferred over broiler chickens for making chicken soup because of their rich flavor in the chicken broth.

- Stock has higher collagen content than broth, which produces a better base for sauces and soups.

- This is a great stock to can using a pressure canner.

Ingredients

3 5-pound whole free-range roasting chickens

3 large yellow onions, unpeeled, quartered

6 carrots, unpeeled, halved

4 celery stalks with leaves, cut in thirds

20 sprigs fresh parsley

15 sprigs fresh thyme

20 sprigs fresh dill

1 head garlic, unpeeled, cut in half crosswise

2 tablespoons kosher salt

2 teaspoons whole black peppercorns

1. Cut chickens into several pieces. Place all ingredients in a large stockpot. Add 7 quarts of water. Bring to a boil and simmer for 6 hours. Turn burner off and let it sit for 1 hour. Strain. Pull the chicken off of the bone and reserve for another use.

2. Place chicken stock in refrigerator overnight. The next day, remove the surface fat. Use immediately or freeze for up to 3 months.

Healthy Chicken Soup

The Perfect Boiled Egg

I have been eating boiled eggs all of my life, but have never found a method of cooking the perfect boiled egg consistently. I tried starting the eggs in hot water, starting with cold water, keeping the water at a simmer after reaching a boil, turning the stove-top completely off as well as many other methods. Finally, I found a foolproof way to boil an egg!

• Older eggs are better for peeling, but new eggs are better for baking and poaching.

• To determine the age of eggs, place eggs in about five inches of water. If the egg lays flat on the bottom it is very fresh and is good for baking and poaching; if the egg tilts on the bottom it is about 10 days old and is great for boiling; if it floats throw it out.

1. Place the eggs in a medium saucepan and cover with about an inch of cool water.

2. Add 1 tablespoon of salt to the water. This helps the protein in the whites, if they should crack, to quickly coagulate.

3. Cover pot and bring water to a boil. Once you hear the water boiling, turn off the heat and follow the chart below for removing the eggs from the pot.

3 minutes: Soft boiled egg
5 minutes: Soft yolk hard boiled egg
7 minutes: Hard boiled egg
9 minutes: Firm yolk hard boiled egg

4. Once eggs are removed, rinse under cold water for about 2 minutes. Thoroughly crack eggs on kitchen counter, then peel shell starting from the fat side of the egg.

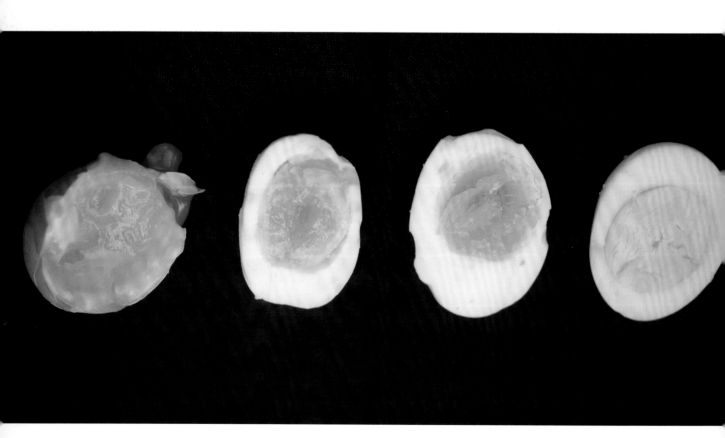

Egg Salad Sandwiches

Serves 6

Egg salad sandwiches always remind me of family reunions and picnics. They are easy to make and are a great make-ahead meal. I like to make a double batch; one for Sunday brunch with a tomato salad and the leftovers for the Monday. I always need an easy lunch and dinner for Mondays.

HINT: If you are not eating these immediately, store them in wax paper in the refrigerator. They will last for about 3 hours.

Ingredients

12 hard boiled eggs, peeled

½ onion, diced

1 cup celery, diced

1 cup pickles, diced

½ cup mayonnaise (preferably homemade, p. 90)

1 tablespoon whole grain mustard

½ teaspoon pepper

Sourdough bread, sliced

½ cup mixed lettuce

1. In a large bowl, smash the eggs with a fork until the whites of the eggs look diced. Stir in the onion, celery, pickles, mayonnaise, mustard, and pepper.
2. Divide egg salad among half the slices of bread. Add the lettuce atop the egg salad. Top with remaining slices of bread.

Perfect Olive Oil Mayonnaise

Yields approximately 1 pint

It seems every time I need mayonnaise, I cannot find a drop in the house. Instead of going to the grocery store I began making this recipe for mayonnaise. Surprisingly, it only took five minutes to prepare and it tasted so fresh, bright, and just plain great!

- Never use aluminum bowls or saucepans to prepare mayonnaise, as they will turn the mayonnaise gray. Store it in plastic, glass, or stainless steel.

- Use the freshest available eggs possible.

- All ingredients must be at room temperature.

Ingredients

1 egg
2 egg yolks
1 teaspoon Dijon mustard
1½ tablespoons Meyer lemon juice
½ teaspoon salt
¼ teaspoon white pepper
2 cups olive oil

1. In a food processor add egg, egg yolks, lemon juice, mustard, salt, and white pepper.

2. Start food processor and run continuously while very slowly adding drops of oil waiting 10 seconds between each drop. Continue with the drops for about ¼ cup of oil.

3. When mayonnaise has definitely thickened add oil in a stream. You may not need all the oil at this time, therefore check after each ½ cup is added for thickness and taste. If the consistency of mayonnaise is very thick, add a drop of lemon to thin it or if too thin add more oil.

4. Place mayonnaise in a bowl and serve or keep covered in refrigerator for one week.

Southern Style Eggs Benedict with Hollandaise Sauce

Serves 4

This scrumptious dish is a perfect brunch on a warm sunny day. With its laid-back quality, it would be welcome for a casual or a celebratory meal.

• Use frozen biscuits to cut down on cooking time.

Ingredients

12 fresh asparagus spears, trimmed
Kosher salt and freshly ground pepper
8 slices of bacon
4 biscuits cut in half (p. 92)
4 eggs
Hollandaise sauce (p. 92)
Olive oil, for drizzling

1. Preheat oven to 425 degrees. Place asparagus on cookie sheet. Drizzle with olive oil and season with salt and pepper. Bake for about 5 minutes or until asparagus is tender.

2. Meanwhile, in a large sauté pan over medium high heat, fry 8 slices of bacon. Remove bacon to a paper towel and all but about 3 tablespoons of bacon drippings.

3. Prepare hollandaise sauce and set aside.

4. Reheat bacon renderings on medium heat. Slowly and carefully crack eggs into sauté pan with the bacon drippings. Cook over medium until whites are almost opaque. Put lid on sauté pan. Cook until whites are opaque. Season with a pinch of salt and pepper.

5. While eggs cook, divide sliced biscuits among four plates. Place two bacon slices across the sliced biscuit, then layer asparagus, Hollandaise sauce and then top with egg. Repeat three more times with remaining ingredients. Serve immediately.

Hollandaise Sauce

Yields 1 cup

Hollandaise sauce is an absolute must for Eggs Benedict. It can be quite finicky and is difficult to reheat, but I think very worthwhile to make. The benefits of this sauce far outweigh the costs. Once you master the sauce, the applications for its use are endless.

HINT: If sauce is too thick add a little more lemon juice.

• Serve Hollandaise sauce over fish, steaks, chicken, and vegetables.

Ingredients

4 egg yolks	1 tablespoon water	Pinch of salt
1 tablespoon lemon juice	½ cup unsalted butter (1 stick), room temperature	Pinch cayenne pepper

1. In a medium sized sauce pan, whisk together egg yolks, water, and lemon juice until thick and light yellow. Over low heat, continue mixing fairly quickly. Try not to let the egg yolks cook too fast. You may have to remove it from the heat source every once in a while. The eggs should become frothy and double in volume.

2. Once mixture has doubled in volume and the eggs are smooth, add a tablespoon of soft butter. Whisk continually to emulsify.

3. Add another tablespoon of butter and so on until the sauce has thickened to the consistency you desire. You may not need to use all of the butter.

4. Season with salt and cayenne pepper. Taste and adjust the seasoning. Serve lukewarm.

Homemade Biscuits

Serves 8-12

HINT: Keep shortening in freezer to keep cold.

Ingredients

3 cups flour plus enough for dusting	¾ teaspoon salt	1 cup buttermilk
1 tablespoon baking powder	½ cup (1 stick) butter, cold	
½ teaspoon baking soda	3 tablespoons shortening, cold	

1. Preheat oven to 425 degrees.

2. In a large bowl, mix dry ingredients together.

3. Cut butter into pea-size pieces. Work shortening and butter into the dry ingredients until incorporated. It should resemble an oatmeal texture. Be careful not to over-mix or the texture will be affected.

4. Pour buttermilk into mixture and mix until just combined. Place dough onto lightly floured surface and fold on top of itself for about 1 minute. Roll dough to 1½-inch thickness. Cut into 3- to 4-inch rounds.

5. Place on Silpat or greased cookie sheet. Make sure the biscuits are touching each other. Put a light thumbprint in center of each biscuit to keep them even when rising.

6. Place in oven for 20 minutes or until golden brown. Halfway through baking lightly brush with melted butter and bake for the remaining 10 minutes. Serve immediately.

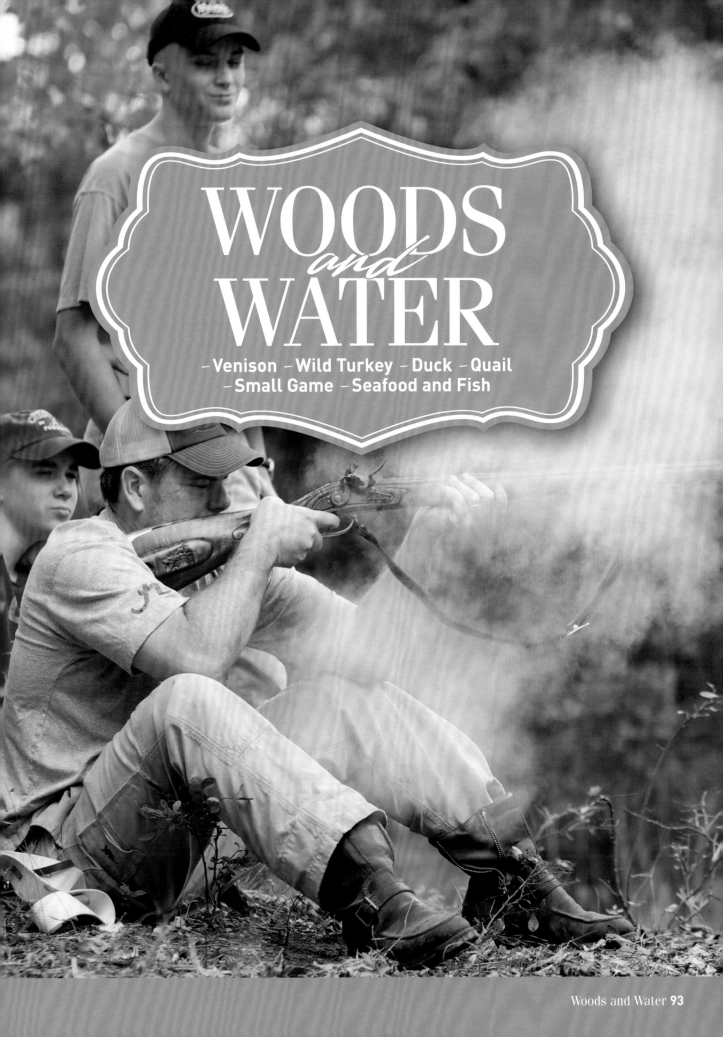

WOODS *and* WATER

– Venison – Wild Turkey – Duck – Quail
– Small Game – Seafood and Fish

Venison

I often hear people say that venison is "tough and has a gamey taste". I have to admit that the first half of my life, I thought the same way. I had only eaten venison once at a wild game supper and it was pretty horrible to say the least. Then.... I met Scott. My life and dining habits from then on would be drastically different. He always kept our freezer full of wild game and as my sons came along, we have had to buy more freezers to keep up with the amount of venison harvested each year. I have loved living off of the harvested venison and enjoy the exceptional depth of flavor that it offers not to mention not having to buy meat at the supermarket.

There are a few reasons for the tough texture and gamey taste of venison. Deer, unlike domesticated cattle, have to rely on the vegetation in the wild for survival and on average are older when harvested. They are lean from their diet and exercise, therefore do not have the marbling of fat that beef contains. Although this makes the deer healthier, it also can cause the meat to be tough if it is not prepared properly. The deer's diet along with improper aging will cause venison to taste gamey. Venison does have a distinct flavor just as grass-fed beef has a distinct flavor and this must not be confused with gaminess. Most domestic-raised animals are bred to be tasteless and fatty. Venison has much more depth of flavor than beef and if properly prepared will be incredibly and delectably tender.

If a walk-in cooler is not available, it is best to quickly process your venison, then allow the meat to age in the refrigerator on a rack, not allowing it to sit in its blood, for five to seven days. Once it has been aged, package the cuts of meat in a double wrap of butcher paper or vacuum sealed bags, then label and date the packages. If you have a walk-in freezer, hang it and leave it for seven to ten days. Following these simple steps should rid the venison of any undesirable gamey flavors.

I prepare the various cuts of venison using different methods. Just as our ancestors before us, I braise the shoulder and neck and use them in stews and soups, brown the loin in a super hot skillet and serve it rare, and prepare the hindquarter roast in a diversity of ways. Since venison does not have much fat, I add healthy fats such as olive oil when I brown the meat. This adds necessary fat to produce a more tender and juicy result.

Additional to the exceptional taste of venison, the health benefits far outweigh those of beef. Not only is deer a free-ranging consumer of healthy herbs, grasses, acorns, berries, and nuts and exempt from harmful antibiotics and hormones, its meat is lower in fat and cholesterol and is higher in vitamin B6, B12, and Omega 3 fatty acids. Many people are choosing to take their health in to their own hands beginning with the foods they eat. They are paying high prices to obtain naturally grass fed meat and many are hunting to acquire meat for their tables in the natural state that God intended.

I find that preparing for and hunting wild game has contributed to the closeness of our family. As our family plans the hunt, prepare the fields, and plant nutritious vegetation for the animals in the wild, much fun, conversation, and ideas abound. Each person contributes to the family›s sustenance whether it is to gather or hunt, or whether it is to prepare and cook the venison. It is all an adventure for every age whether male, female, old, or young. There are no phones, gadgets, or distractions; just you, the kids, and the great outdoors. After the meal is prepared, the stories come to life of the hunt, and all the preparation and hard work together is rewarded with a delicious, succulent meal. Enjoy your family as you begin or continue the family traditions of planning, working, hunting, and enjoying the outdoors and the incredible food that you harvest together.

• Venison is that meat of any game animal, especially that of a deer. My venison recipes are suitable to whitetail, red deer, fallow deer, moose, caribou, and pronghorn antelope.

Substitutions

All venison recipes succeed using beef, but not all beef recipes succeed using venison.

There are many of you reading this book who do not hunt. Do not let that stop you from using the recipes in this book calling for wild game. There are substitutions that will come pretty close to the rich flavor of the proteins that are harvested from the wild. With any of your proteins, always choose grass-fed organic animals and the beautiful earthy flavors will come through. Animals with a variety in their diets always taste better than those fed purely from corn or grain. My desire is that you get maximum health and flavor from your carefully chosen meats and that you never stop experimenting with your cuisine.

Venison

In most recipes, the venison can be replaced with grass-fed beef, goat, or lamb. The best cuts of meat for the various type recipes are as follows:

Venison tenderloin — beef tenderloin or loin
Venison loin — beef loin
Venison hindquarter roast

Flank steak is a good substitute for venison hindquarter roast if the recipe instructs you to pound the meat, use in stir fries or burritos, or instructs you to slice the meat horizontally and sear.

Beef, goat, or lamb stew meat is a good substitute venison hindquarter roast if used in recipes that instruct you to braise, such as in stews and soups.

Wild Turkey

Domestic turkey may be substituted for wild turkey. The flavor will not be as intense, but it is a good substitute.

Wild Duck

Domestic duck may be substituted for wild duck. Remove the fat from the domestic duck, in that wild duck does not have the fat content that is found in domestic ducks.

Domestic Poultry

Farm-raised poultry may be substituted for domestic poultry, but the flavor will not be as intense and you will need to cut the cooking time by two-thirds.

You may substitute 2 pheasants in place of domestic poultry. You can find pheasant at high-end supermarkets.

Quail

Farm-raised quail are a great substitute for wild quail. They can be found in the freezer sections of high-end supermarkets. If your store does not have them, speak with the meat manager and he will probably order some for you.

Ragu Bolognese

Serves 4 to 6

There are some great dishes you can make ahead of time, freeze, and use when convenient. Bolognese is one of these dishes. I like to make a triple batch of the sauce, have some for dinner, and freeze the other two batches for another time.

Ingredients

¼ cup extra virgin olive oil

2 medium onions, finely chopped

4 ribs celery, finely chopped

2 carrots, finely chopped

4 cloves garlic, sliced

1 pound ground venison

1 pound ground beef

4 ounces slab bacon, finely chopped

2 16-ounce cans of tomatoes, crushed (preferably homemade)

2 tablespoons tomato paste

1 teaspoon fresh thyme leaves

1 cup dry red wine

½ cup heavy cream

¼ teaspoon nutmeg

Kosher salt and freshly ground pepper

1 box Fettuccine noodles

½ cup Parmesan cheese, plus extra for serving

1. Heat olive oil in a heavy-bottomed pot over medium heat until hot. Add the onions, celery, carrots, and garlic and cook for 5 minutes or until vegetables are translucent.

2. Increase the heat and add venison, beef, and bacon, stirring often.

3. Add tomatoes, tomato paste, wine, and thyme. Bring to a boil, then lower to a simmer for 1 hour.

4. Meanwhile, bring a large pot of water to a boil. Add 1 tablespoon of oil and 1 tablespoon of salt to the water. Add Fettuccine to the water for about 12 minutes or until al dente.

5. Add heavy cream and nutmeg to the sauce. Simmer about 8 to 10 minutes. Season with salt and pepper to taste. Remove from heat, and let cool.

6. When the pasta is cooked, drain and place the noodles on 4 to 6 plates. Top the pasta with the sauce. Divide the Parmesan cheese among the plates and serve.

Stuffed Venison Loin

Serves 8

Stuffed venison loin is a tender, tasty, easy, elegant dish. It is perfect for special occasions. It's very versatile in taste. You could add mushrooms, different cheeses and herbs to the stuffing. It allows for creativity in a consistent no-fail dish!

Ingredients

1 loin, halved butterflied (p. 98)
½ cup breadcrumbs
¾ cup shredded mozzarella cheese
1 cup Parmesan cheese
½ cup olive oil
½ cup chopped basil leaves
2 garlic cloves, minced
Salt
Pepper

1. In a medium sized bowl, mix together breadcrumbs, cheeses, olive oil, basil, and garlic.

2. Pre-heat oven to 350 degrees. Butterfly the two loins.

3. Spread filling evenly over the two pounded loins. Roll up the loins and truss (p. 98).

4. Liberally sprinkle with salt and pepper. Place in smoking hot cast iron skillet. Brown loins on all sides. Place loins in 350-degree oven for 3 to 4 minutes. Remove from pan. Let rest. Slice into 1-inch pieces. Serve with homemade mashed potatoes, rice, carrots, green beans, or salad.

HOW TO:
BUTTERFLY A LOIN

Step 1

With a long sharp knife on the right half of the loin, slice loin two-thirds of the way through.

Step 2

Turn the loin over and repeat.

Step 3

Spread out sliced loin.

Step 4

Pound the loin to about ¼-inch thick.

HOW TO:
TRUSS A LOIN

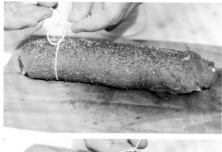

Step 1

Spread stuffing on top of pounded loin leaving a ½-inch border around the edges. Gently roll loin into a log and begin to truss. Using butcher's twine about 6 times longer than your loin, wrap around loin approximately 1½ inches from end and tie a knot.

Step 2

Hold the short end of the twine above the knot with your left hand. Pull the long end of the twine away from you and slip it under the part of the twine that you are holding taut above the loin. Repeat wrapping process every 1½ to 2 inches until entire loin is trussed.

Step 3

Turn the loin over and stretch the twine around the end, wrapping around each truss until it reaches the first initial truss. Tie ends together and trim excess.

Easy Venison Chili Con Carne

Serves 6 to 8

Everyone has his or her favorite chili recipe, and this is my family's favorite. Venison chili adds a depth of flavor that is superior to other kinds of meats. President Johnson knew this and it is noted that he requested the cooks at the White House to use only venison for his chili. The corn mix in this recipe adds an earthy flavor and adds a texture that is perfect for Con Carne.

Ingredients

- 1 16-ounce can of tomatoes, diced
- 1 tablespoon minced canned chipotle chili in adobe sauce
- 5 slices bacon, finely chopped
- 4 pounds venison stew meat, cut into ½-inch cubes
- Pepper and Kosher salt

- 2 tablespoons olive oil
- 1 large onion, chopped
- 1 jalapeno chili, seeded and chopped
- 1 can kidney beans
- 3 tablespoons chili powder
- 1½ teaspoons ground cumin

- 1½ teaspoon oregano
- 4 garlic cloves, minced
- 4 cups beef broth
- 1 tablespoon packed brown sugar
- 2 tablespoons yellow corn muffin mix

• Always make sure your venison is dry and the skillet is super hot before you brown the meat. Browning enhances the flavor of the dish by giving more depth of flavor.

1. In a food processor, place tomatoes and chipotle chili and puree until smooth (This should only take about 10 seconds). In a Dutch oven, cook the bacon over medium heat until crisp. Transfer bacon to paper towel. Leave the fat in the pan.

2. Pat venison dry and season with salt and pepper. Heat the fat until smoking hot. Brown half of the venison. (Do not crowd the pan or the meat will steam instead of brown). This should take about 6 minutes. Using a slotted spoon, transfer to bowl and repeat.

3. Add the olive oil, onions, and jalapeño to Dutch oven and cook for about 5 minutes or until softened. Stir in kidney beans, chili powder, cumin, oregano, and garlic.

4. Cook for about 30 seconds. Stir in broth, tomato mixture and brown sugar and bring to a boil. Reduce heat to low and simmer, covered, for 1 hour. Uncover and simmer for about 30 minutes longer.

5. Ladle 1 cup chili liquid into medium-sized bowl and stir in yellow corn muffin mix. Whisk mixture into chili and simmer until chili thickens. Check seasonings. Serve with a dollop of sour cream or cheese and Jalapeno Cornbread (p. 33).

Venison Burrito Supreme

Venison Burrito Supreme

Serves 4

This recipe is not only one of the tastiest burrito recipes I have eaten, it is healthy as well. My family devours these burritos the minute they are made. These burritos are easy to make, and if you are having a party everyone can have fun creating their own! Be sure to double the Tomatillo Sauce and the Pico de Gallo and use it for chip dipping.

Ingredients

4 tablespoons olive oil
4 garlic cloves
1½ teaspoons red pepper flakes
1 can black beans (16 oz.) with juice
1 pound venison hindquarter
Salt and pepper to taste
1½ cups cooked rice
4 flour tortillas
6 tablespoons chopped cilantro
Tomatillo sauce (p. 58)

Pico de Gallo Ingredients

2 tablespoons chopped cilantro
4 plum tomatoes, cored and chopped
½ red onion, minced
1 jalapeno chili, seeded and minced
1 tablespoon lime juice
Salt and pepper to taste

1. Combine Pico de Gallo ingredients in medium bowl and season with salt and pepper. Set aside.

2. Heat 2 tablespoons of olive oil in large saucepan over medium-high heat until just smoking. Add garlic and red pepper flakes and brown for about 30 seconds. Add beans, bring to a boil, and then reduce it to a simmer for about 15 minutes. Season with salt and pepper.

3. Meanwhile, prepare the tomatillo sauce.

4. Slice hindquarter venison in half horizontally. Pound each half to about ¾ inches thick. Season liberally with salt and pepper. Heat oil in a large skillet over medium high heat until skillet is smoking hot. Place venison in skillet for about 4 minutes on the first side, turn and cook the other side for 3 to 4 minutes. Transfer to a cutting board, tent with foil, and let rest 5 minutes.

5. Slice steaks thinly against the grain. Place tortillas on 4 plates and evenly divide rice, beans, venison, and Pico de Gallo among them. Fold tortillas to form burritos. Spoon Tomatillo sauce on top of burrito and garnish with cilantro. Serve immediately.

Cocoa Crusted Venison With Berry Reduction

Serves 6

Chocolate is amazingly awesome with venison, believe it or not. Well, chocolate on almost anything is irresistible. I knew Scott was the man for me when he was able to resist Alaskan chocolate covered berries after losing 20 pounds in two weeks on an Alaskan hunting trip just to bring me my favorite ingredient and treat!

• It is known that melting chocolate in your mouth increases brain activity and prevents potential brain problems in the elderly.

Ingredients

⅓ cup coffee grounds

¼ cup cocoa

2½ tablespoons salt

1 tablespoon brown sugar

1 teaspoon cinnamon

½ teaspoon cayenne pepper

2 tenderloins

Olive oil for browning

1. Preheat oven to 350 degrees.

2. In a medium-sized bowl, mix coffee grounds, cocoa, salt, brown sugar, cinnamon, and cayenne pepper in a bowl. Rub mixture into loins.

3. Heat olive oil in a cast iron skillet to almost smoking. Place loins into skillet and brown on all sides.

4. Place loins in 350 degree oven 4 to 5 minutes, depending on size of loins. Remove to a cutting board. Let rest for at least 5 minutes.

5. Slice loins and spoon berry reduction on top of venison. Serve with collard greens.

Berry Reduction

Ingredients

1½ cups blackberries

½ cup blueberries

½ cup red wine (Cabernet Sauvignon)

¼ cup sugar

1 lemon, juiced

Kosher salt, to taste

1. Place blackberries, blueberries, red wine, sugar, and lemon juice in a small saucepan and bring to a boil. Reduce the heat to simmer and reduce by half. Season with salt.

Cocoa Crusted Venison With Berry Reduction

Beer-Braised Venison with Turnips, Onions, and Carrots

Serves 4 to 6

During hunting season, we always plant turnips in our green fields for the deer. The great thing about this is that we enjoy cooking them with the game we harvest! Not only are there many gastronomic benefits of turnips, the health benefits seem endless. Turnips are filled with antioxidants, are rich in vitamins C, A, K, B, folic acid, and carotenoids. Next time you feel a cold coming on, eat some turnips and enjoy this hearty tasty stew.

Ingredients

1 pound venison hindquarter roast

½ teaspoon freshly ground black pepper

1½ tablespoons salt

½ cup all-purpose flour

3 tbsp. olive oil

1 cup beef broth

4 garlic cloves, crushed

1 (12 ounce) bottle dark beer

2 bay leaves

4 carrots, peeled and cut diagonally into ½-inch thick slices

10 ounces small turnips, peeled and cut into wedges

1 large onion, peeled and cut into wedges

¼ cup chopped fresh flat-leaf parsley

1. Cut hindquarter into 1-inch cubes. Place them in a medium sized bowl. Sprinkle salt and pepper liberally over meat. Mix well. Coat the meat with the flour.

2. Heat oil in a Dutch oven. When smoking hot, brown meat on all sides. Do not crowd the pan; if necessary, brown meat in batches.

3. Add beef broth, beer, garlic cloves, and bay leaves. Scrape the browned bits off of the bottom of the pan and bring to a boil.

4. Add carrots, turnips, and onion to Dutch oven. Bring to a boil. Once it reaches a boil, bring heat down to a simmer and cook covered for about an hour.

5. Sprinkle parsley on top and serve over mashed potatoes with crusty bread.

Moroccan Venison Shepherd's Pie

Serves 4

Sweet potatoes are about the easiest vegetables in the world to grow if you can keep the deer away from them. During late summer, does with fawns find them irresistible. The Moroccan spices and the sweet potatoes make this dish flavorful and exciting.

Ingredients

2 tablespoons olive oil

1½ pounds venison hindquarter, cut into 1-inch cubes

½ teaspoon roasted ground cumin

½ teaspoon kosher salt

1 onion, chopped

4 cloves garlic, minced

1 tablespoon tomato paste

2 cups beef broth

⅓ cup black olives

⅓ cup raisins

3 tablespoons honey

½ teaspoon ground red pepper

¼ teaspoon ground turmeric

½ teaspoon cinnamon, divided

1 cup frozen green peas

4 cups sweet potatoes, peeled and chopped

1 large egg, lightly beaten

1. Preheat oven to 350 degrees.

2. Heat oil in a medium-sized skillet over medium-high heat. Sprinkle venison with cumin and salt. Add venison to the pan and brown for about 1 minute on each side. Remove venison from the pan. Add onions and sauté for 3 minutes. Add garlic for about 30 seconds, and then add the tomato paste. Stir well.

3. Add broth to the pan. Bring to a boil, scraping pan to loosen the browned bits. Stir in olives, raisins, honey, ground red pepper, turmeric, and one half of the cinnamon. Add venison back to the pan. Reduce heat, and simmer 30 minutes. Remove from heat and stir in the peas.

4. Meanwhile, cook sweet potatoes in a pot of boiling water until tender and drain. Sprinkle with a pinch of salt and the rest of the cinnamon. Beat potatoes with a mixer and add egg. Continue mixing until well combined. Spoon venison mixture evenly into 4 ramekins, and then spread potato mixture over the venison mixture. Place ramekins on a baking sheet and bake at 350 degrees for 30 minutes or until bubbly.

Western Venison Open-Faced Sandwich with Fried Egg

Serves 4

On our honeymoon, we went skiing in Jackson Hole, Wyoming. What an adventure. We loved the food, and both of us gained about 10 pounds that week. One thing that I noticed was that most of the restaurants had some kind of wild game on their menu, namely venison. That amazed me. I thought cooking venison was just what "good ole' boy" Southern hunters cooked. I never knew that it could be an *elegant delicacy*. The other thing I noticed was that it was expensive: *People wanted it*. I was inspired to learn how to make it a delicacy in my home. One morning, we had breakfast at this awesome restaurant where we had to wait about two hours to get in. I loved this dish and wanted to replicate it at home. I think I've got it pretty close.

Marinade Ingredients

¼ cup Rosemary

¼ cup Thyme

½ cup olive oil

3 cloves garlic

Venison Ingredients

1½ pounds venison hindquarter roast, sliced in half horizontally

4 tablespoons olive oil, extra for browning

1 Vidalia onion, chopped

2 cloves of garlic

1 pound tomatoes, peeled or canned with their juices

1 tablespoon tomato paste

3 tablespoons fresh basil, chopped

Kosher salt

Freshly ground pepper

4 eggs

4 slices of artisan bread, cut ½ inch thick, toasted or grilled

4 tablespoons Parmesan Reggiano cheese

¼ cup Parsley

1. For marinade, mix rosemary, thyme, olive oil, garlic and venison in a zip-top bag and refrigerate 4 hours.

2. Remove venison from refrigerator and pound each half to ¾ inch thick. Season liberally with salt and pepper. Heat 2 tablespoons of olive oil in a medium- size skillet over medium-high heat until skillet is almost smoking and oil is shimmering. Place venison in skillet for about 4 minutes on the first side, then turn over and cook for 3 to 4 more minutes. Transfer to cooling rack and allow to rest.

3. Meanwhile, heat 2 tablespoons of oil in a medium sized saucepan over medium-high heat. Add onions and garlic and stir for 30 seconds. Add tomatoes, tomato paste, basil, ½ teaspoon of salt, and ¼ teaspoon of pepper. Bring mixture to a boil, then reduce it to a simmer for about 15 minutes.

4. Halve each piece of toast on the bias and drizzle with olive oil. Place toast on the plates.

5. Slice venison against the grain and distribute equally over the toast. Spoon about ¼ cup of the tomato mixture over the venison.

6. Heat 2 tablespoons of olive oil in a large non-stick skillet over medium heat. Add 2 eggs at one time to the pan. Cover and cook at medium to medium-low heat for 2–3 minutes or until whites are set, but yolk is still soft. Gently remove the eggs from the skillet and place over the tomatoes. Repeat with remaining eggs.

7. Sprinkle 1 tablespoon of Parmesan Reggiano cheese over each egg. Garnish with Parsley and serve immediately.

Western Venison Open-Faced Sandwich with Fried Egg

Venison Scaloppine

Serves 6

Scaloppine is an elegant but simple dish to prepare. The flavor and texture of venison prepared as scaloppine can't be matched.

Ingredients:

1½ pounds venison loin

2 cups all purpose flour

2 teaspoons kosher salt

1 teaspoon freshly ground black pepper

3 extra large eggs

Olive oil

2 cups breadcrumbs, dried and seasoned

Olive oil, for frying

1 pound large button mushrooms, quartered

1½ cups sherry or marsala wine

4 tablespoons cold unsalted butter

3 tablespoons fresh thyme leaves

• Make a double match of the fried venison, freeze one batch on sheet pans until frozen, then store it in freezer bags. When ready to use it, remove from freezer and place on a baking sheet and bake at 200 degrees until warmed through. Meanwhile, prepare the sauce and serve with your favorite crusty bread.

1. Slice venison into 1-inch pieces. Pound to ¼ inch thick.

2. On a plate, mix together flour, salt, and pepper. On a second plate, beat the eggs with 1 tablespoon of water. On a third plate, add the breadcrumbs.

3. Lightly dredge venison in the flour mixture, then the eggs, and lastly the breadcrumbs.

4. Heat olive oil and half the butter in a large cast iron skillet or sauté pan. Cook about 2 minutes over medium heat on each side or until brown. Transfer pieces of venison to a cooling rack.

5. Add a little more olive oil and the mushrooms to the pan until juices have been absorbed. Add sherry to mushrooms and reduce by half. Add remaining butter to the pan and bring just to a boil. Lower the heat to medium and cook for about 5 more minutes.

6. Stir in the thyme leaves. Pour mushrooms and sauce over the venison and serve.

Stuffed Venison Meatloaf

Serves 6

This dish is so beautiful in its presentation that it's hard to call it a comfort meal. It's one of the most elegant and easy comfort dishes that I've ever made, and is always a winner in our home.

Ingredients

2 teaspoons olive oil

1 onion, chopped

2 garlic cloves, chopped

2 carrots, julienned

1 pound ground venison

1 pound ground lean beef

2 cups breadcrumbs

1 cup Parmesan Reggiano Cheese

2 teaspoons Dijon mustard

3 large eggs, lightly beaten

1 tablespoon kosher salt

½ tablespoon pepper

15-20 spinach leaves

4 ounces mozzarella cheese, thinly sliced

10 slices bacon

1. Preheat oven to 400 degrees. Heat olive oil in 10-inch skillet over medium heat. Put onions into skillet and sweat the onions until softened. Add garlic and cook for 30 seconds.

2. Bring a stockpot of water to a boil. Add carrots to the water and boil them for 8 minutes. Drain and set aside.

3. In a large bowl, combine ground venison, beef, breadcrumbs, softened onions, garlic, Parmesan Reggiano, Dijon mustard, eggs, salt and pepper.

4. On a Silpat or piece of wax paper form the meat mixture into a 10-inch × 16-inch rectangle that is ½ inch thick. Lay the spinach leaves over the meat leaving a ½-inch border around the perimeter of the rectangle. Layer Mozzarella slices on top of spinach leaves and then lay the carrots lengthwise on top of the Mozzarella. Roll the meat lengthwise (starting with long side) making it as tight as possible. Pick up Silpat or wax paper and roll the loaf onto a rack that is placed on top of a half sheet pan with sides.

5. Slice bacon in half and place width wise over the loaf. Bake for 1 hour or until loaf reaches 165 degrees.

6. Transfer the meatloaf to a cutting board. Cut meatloaf into 1-inch slices and serve with Garlic Mashed Potatoes (p. 34), salad, and crusty bread.

Venison Sausage

Venison Sausage Smothered in Italian Tomatoes and Onions Over Cheesy Grits

Serves 8

What better comfort food for the Southerner than sausage and grits with an onion and tomato reduction? The creamy grits and spicy venison link sausage bring back the calm gentle days of childhood and give me the desire to create the same memories for future generations. This recipe will hopefully stay in my family as well as yours as a keepsake. This sausage recipe can be used for sausage patties as well as link sausage. Lasagna, spaghetti, or Bolognese can be greatly enhanced by using the sausage part of this recipe.

Many people think of sausage and grits as a winter time meal, but chilies and spicy dishes always have been used in the heat to cause perspiration to cool oneself down. Fresh tomatoes picked right off the vine can't be matched for taste and freshness during the hot southern summer. This is a dish you will love to eat anytime of the year.

HINT: You can use any cut of the deer for this recipe.

Sausage Ingredients

4 pounds venison scraps, run through the largest holes of grinder.

2 pounds of lean bacon, run through the same grinder.

1 tablespoon kosher salt

½ tablespoon pepper

½ tablespoon red pepper flakes

1 tablespoon rosemary, minced

½ cup Italian parsley

½ cup dry white wine

8 ounces sausage casings (about 8 feet)

1. In a large bowl, mix the venison and bacon with your hands until well blended. Add the rest of the ingredients and mix just until blended. Chill mixture for 30 minutes.

2. Set up a sausage stuffer and attach the casing to the funnel feeder. Begin stuffing the sausage into the casing and twist every 6 inches. Keep the diameter about 1 inch to ensure proper cooking. Prick sausage with a pin all over. Chill until ready to cook.

Tomato and Onion Sauce Ingredients

3 tablespoons extra virgin olive oil

1 medium yellow onion, ½-inch diced

2 cloves garlic, minced

2 tablespoons tomato paste

½ cup chicken stock

1 cup red wine

¼ cup Italian parsley

1. Heat 2 tablespoons of olive oil in 10- to 12-inch sauté pan. Add half the sausage links to the pan. Cook over low heat, turning frequently, until browned on all sides. Transfer to a plate. Brown remaining sausage links and transfer to plate.

2. Pour 1 tablespoon olive oil in the same pan sausage was cooked. Add onions and garlic to the pan and cook until soft, 8 to 10 minutes.

3. In a small bowl mix tomato paste, stock, and red wine. Add mixture to the pan. Scrape brown bits from the bottom of the pan and bring to a simmer.

4. Return sausage to the pan, cover, and cook for 15 minutes or until cooked through. Stir in parsley and serve over Cheesy Grits (p. 83).

Venison Sausage Patties

Serves 8

I love waking up to the smell of sausage in the kitchen. Scott is actually an excellent cook and allows me to "sleep in" on the weekends. Often, I awake to an incredible breakfast of venison sausage and biscuits served with spicy mustard! Who could ask for more? One secret to this recipe is using prosciutto. Prosciutto is fully smoked, adds great flavor and allows you to cook the patties medium as opposed to well-done.

HINT: If your venison is already ground, just chop the prosciutto in very small pieces and add to your ground venison.

Ingredients

4 pounds of venison scraps (you could use any part of the deer for this recipe), run through the largest holes of the meat grinder.

2 pounds of prosciutto run through the same grinder. Have your butcher run it through his grinder if you do not have one of your own.

1 tablespoon salt

½ tablespoon pepper

½ tablespoon red pepper flakes

½ cup dry white wine

2 tablespoons extra virgin olive oil

1. In a large bowl, mix venison and prosciutto with your hands until blended. Add salt, pepper, red pepper flakes, and white wine. Chill for about 30 minutes.

2. Form sausage into 4-ounce patties. Do not over-handle the mix as this can affect the texture of the sausage.

3. Heat olive oil in a 10- or 12-inch cast iron skillet. Add sausage patties and cook over low heat, turning frequently, until light brown on all sides. Cook in batches. Serve with Homemade Biscuits (p. 92).

Venison Lettuce Wraps

On days I feel like having a light meal I prepare these little jewels. They are so full of flavor and texture. You get salty, sweet and crunch! The kids start piling into the kitchen as the aromas of the dish reach their noses. The wraps hardly make it to the table.

• Peanut oil has a high heat tolerance. The oil is less likely to burn at high temperatures.

• To make this dish extra special, fry some rice sticks in peanut oil until puffed and serve on top of lettuce wraps. They can be found in the Asian aisle of the grocery store.

Ingredients

1 pound venison hindquarter, diced into ½-inch cubes
2 tablespoons soy sauce
1 teaspoon red pepper flakes
1 tablespoon hoisin sauce
2 tablespoons lemon juice
¼ cup peanut oil
2 cups diced water chestnuts
½ cup diced white onions

1 cup diced green onions
1 garlic clove, smashed
1 teaspoon fresh-smashed ginger
1 tablespoon seasoned rice wine vinegar
3 tablespoons soy sauce
3 tablespoons chicken stock
1 head iceberg lettuce, washed and separated

1. Mix soy sauce, red pepper flakes, hoisin sauce, and lemon juice in a medium bowl. Marinate venison in mixture for 20 minutes.

2. Heat peanut oil in a wok. When oil is shimmering add half of the marinated meat and brown. Transfer first batch of meat to a plate and repeat with remaining half.

3. Add water chestnuts, white onions, green onions, garlic, and ginger to wok for 2 to 3 minutes.

4. Add vinegar, soy sauce, and chicken stock and cook until caramelized.

5. Place venison in the wok with the onion mixture. Mix well.

6. Serve wrapped in lettuce leaves.

Venison Korean Wraps

Serves 6

I love the flavors in these super wraps! The spicy, salty, flavor of the venison paired with the sweet cabbage dressing and Taco Sauce is perfectly balanced. The cabbage adds just enough crunch and texture to make this dish absolutely addictive.

Ingredients

8 tablespoons soy sauce, divided

6 teaspoons toasted sesame oil, divided

1½ teaspoons salt

¼ teaspoon pepper

soy sauce

4 tablespoons honey, divided

2 tablespoons lime juice

2 tablespoons hoisin sauce

1 tablespoon red pepper paste

1 teaspoon rice wine vinegar

2 garlic cloves, smashed

1½ pounds venison hindquarter, sliced in half horizontally

12 mini flour tortillas

4 cups shredded iceberg lettuce

¼ cup shredded Napa cabbage

¼ cup shredded red cabbage

10 scallions, sliced on the bias

1. For marinade, combine 5 tablespoons soy sauce, 2 teaspoons of sesame oil, salt, and pepper in a medium bowl. Coat the venison with the marinade. Cover and refrigerate for at least 1 hour.

2. Meanwhile, prepare the Cabbage Dressing and the Korean Taco Sauce. For the Cabbage Dressing, combine 1 tablespoon soy sauce, 1 tablespoon honey, 2 teaspoons sesame oil, and lime juice in a large bowl. Mix well and set aside.

3. For the Korean Taco Sauce, combine 2 tablespoons soy sauce, the 3 remaining tablespoons honey, 2 teaspoons sesame oil, hoisin sauce, red pepper paste, rice wine vinegar, and garlic in a medium bowl.

4. Remove venison from refrigerator. Heat cast iron skillet until smoking hot, and then add both pieces of venison. Brown for 3 minutes. Turn over for another 2 to 3 minutes until medium rare. Transfer venison to a cutting board and let rest.

5. Meanwhile, place 3 tortillas in a large, dry, non-stick skillet over medium-high heat until pliable, about 20 seconds per side. Repeat with remaining tortillas.

6. Add lettuce, cabbage, and scallions to bowl with Cabbage Dressing. Toss to combine. Add salt and pepper to taste.

7. Cut venison into strips across the bias.

8. Fill tortillas with cabbage mixture, venison, and drizzle with Korean Taco Sauce.

TIP: Scallions are re-usable! By re-usable, I mean that they actually can be used at least twice. After the first cutting of the green hollow part of the onion, you can place the white portion in about 2 inches of water and place them in a sunny window seal then watch them take off growing. Change the water daily and you will find that they grow very quickly, about an inch a day.

The white part of the scallion is used for medicinal purposes as well as a culinary purposes. Scallions are used as an anti-septic, an an-antifungal, anti-bacterial, and expectorant. Scallions treat the the respiratory tract therefore treating the common cold. It is hard to believe, but scallions even help indigestion and insomnia. I better go to the garden right now, pull up some scallions and get to munching! Maybe I will get better sleep tonight.

Venison Korean Wraps

Turkey

Turkeys are incredibly friendly. We have two turkeys that follow us around as if they were dogs. They travel from window to window just to peer inside and be a little closer to us. As I am writing, one turkey is sitting on the top of a rocking chair peering in the window and the other is dozing off to sleep. They garden with us, walk with us, and relax on the porch with us. The hunters in the family have a great respect for these and other wildlife and therefore take responsibility concerning every area of nature and the outdoors.

As much as I enjoy a domestic turkey at Thanksgiving, wild turkey is by far my favorite of the two. They have many differences that affect the flavor of the finished dish. Domestic turkeys cannot fly or run fast. They are bred to have very large breasts and this causes them to be quite unstable and unable to exercise. Wild turkeys are built for survival. They easily fly and are very fast runners, building up quite a lot of muscle and connective tissue. The diet of domestic turkeys is mostly corn and grain while wild turkeys feast on a diverse diet consisting of berries, herbs, grass, and insects. The wild turkeys that the boys bring home are much older than the domestic variety.

Because of all these differences, the size, flavor, and texture of the turkey is greatly affected. Wild turkey will have much more depth of flavor, but if not prepared correctly will be tough. There are many injector kits available to add moisture to the meat if you are frying or roasting the turkey, but my favorite method of cooking wild turkey is to quarter, brown, and braise the pieces. I also love stuffing the breast as well as slicing, pounding, and frying the cutlets. All of these methods break down the connective tissue and muscle fiber, making it so tender that you can easily cut it with a fork. The stock that a turkey carcass provides is excellent as well. There is not much better eating than the wild turkey, a traditional American favorite.

Turkey Cutlets With Mixed Greens and Herb Vinaigrette

Serves 4

There is nothing as flavorful as wild turkey with herb vinaigrette. The tanginess of the Balsamic Vinegar and earthiness of the herbs paired with the buttery, tender goodness of the turkey just melts in your mouth and leaves you craving more. This is one dish that is deliciously unforgettable!

This dish is nice with shaved parmesan as well.

Ingredients

1 turkey breast
1 cup flour
1 tablespoon salt
½ tablespoon pepper
2 eggs
1 tablespoon water
1 cup bread crumbs
4 tablespoons olive oil for frying (divided)
4 tablespoons butter (divided)
4 cups mixed greens
12 cherry tomatoes, halved
1 cup Herb Vinaigrette (p. 49)
2 tablespoons fresh parsley, chopped

1. Cut turkey breast into ¾-inch pieces. Pound to ¼ inch thick with a meat mallet.

2. On a large plate mix flour, salt, and pepper. On a second plate beat eggs and water together. On a third plate place breadcrumbs. Dredge dry pounded turkey breast pieces into seasoned flour mixture, then egg mixture, then breadcrumbs.

3. In a hot sauté pan, melt butter and oil. When sizzling, place turkey in pan and brown for about 2 minutes per side. Cook in batches. Do not crowd the pan. Transfer to a platter and keep warm.

4. In a medium-sized bowl mix greens with ¼ cup vinaigrette. Divide salad among 4 plates. Place a piece of fried turkey on top of greens. Garnish with fresh parsley and cherry tomatoes then drizzle extra vinaigrette as desired.

Quarter-Pound Turkey Burgers

Serves 8

One of my girls said these burgers were the best burgers she had ever eaten. This is the recipe for you if you do not know what to do with turkey thighs. Served with chipotle sauce, these burgers are truly addictive. If you have leftovers (we never do), these patties are great for breakfast with fried eggs and grits. You can also freeze the patties.

• These patties do not shrink much so you do not have to compensate with larger patties.

Ingredients

1 pound ground turkey thighs

1 pound ground pork

4 ounces ground thick-cut bacon,

1½ cups bread crumbs

¼ cup olive oil

¼ cup milk

2 large eggs, lightly beaten

2 tablespoon pepper

1 tablespoon salt

1 tablespoon rosemary, chopped

1 tablespoon basil, chopped

1 tablespoon red pepper flakes

1. Mix all ingredients in a large bowl. Be careful not to overwork the turkey mixture.

2. Prepare ¼ pound balls and flatten to ¾-inch thick patties.

3. Place patties on a griddle or grill on medium high heat. Cook 3 to 5 minutes on each side until cooked through and caramelized on each side. Serve on your favorite bun with your favorite toppings and condiments. In my opinion, Chipotle Dipping Sauce (p. 37) and bacon slices can't be beat!

Stuffed Turkey Breast

Serves 4 to 6

If you ask me, you just can't beat Stuffed Turkey. This dish not only has a beautiful presentation, but also has the flavor punch that my family craves. The aromas of the buttery turkey and herbs will fill your house with warmth. The flavors of the stuffing and the tenderness of the turkey make for a succulent meal for any occasion. I can see this dish served on Christmas night as well as any day of the week!

Ingredients

¼ cup mushrooms, sautéed and chopped

½ cup parmesan cheese, grated

½ cup artichoke hearts

¼ cup parsley, chopped

2 garlic cloves, minced

1 teaspoon kosher salt

½ teaspoon freshly ground pepper

1 pound turkey breast

1. Preheat oven to 350 degrees.

2. Place mushrooms, cheese, artichokes, parsley, garlic, salt, and pepper in a food processor and pulse until blended.

3. Butterfly turkey breast in the same manner as venison loin shown on page 98. Pound turkey breast to ¼ inch thick. You should end up with about a 10 × 6 rectangle.

4. Place artichoke mixture on center of pounded turkey leaving an inch border around the edges. With long side facing you, roll away from you into medium tight cylinder. Truss turkey breast (p. 98).

5. Coat turkey in olive oil. Generously salt and pepper turkey. Place turkey on smoking hot skillet and brown on all sides. Place turkey in oven and bake for about 30 minutes or until turkey registers 140 degrees.

6. Transfer turkey to cutting board and allow to rest for 5 to 10 minutes. Remove twine and slice into ½-inch slices. Serve with rice, asparagus, and crusty bread.

Skewered Wild Turkey

Skewered Wild Turkey with Chili Ginger Dipping Sauce

Serves 10

I served these winning turkey skewers at a wedding party that I gave for my adorable niece. These wild turkey skewers are great for any occasion from weddings to tailgate parties!

HINT: Add snow peas to the mix and serve over rice noodles with a few splashes of low-sodium soy sauce and make this dish into a meal.

Asian Turkey Ingredients

2 tablespoons dark sesame seed oil

2 tablespoons rice wine vinegar

1½ tablespoons garlic, minced

1 tablespoon soy sauce

1 skinless boneless turkey breast

Chili Ginger Dip Ingredients

1½ tablespoons fresh gingerroot, minced

2 tablespoons soy sauce

1 tablespoon rice wine vinegar

3 tablespoons lemon juice

1 teaspoon sesame seed oil

2 tablespoons chili paste

½ cup mayonnaise

Tabasco to taste

1. Cut turkey breast into 1-inch wide slices against the grain of the meat. Pound slices into ¼ inch thickness, then cut pounded pieces into about 1½-inch × 5-inch strips.

2. In a large bowl mix the dark sesame seed oil, rice wine vinegar, garlic, and soy sauce and pour over the turkey. Massage gently into meat. Cover and refrigerate overnight.

3. Thread each piece of marinated turkey onto skewers. Heat griddle or grill until almost smoking. Cook turkey for about 3 minutes, turn over and cook for 2 more minutes.

4. In a medium-sized bowl combine ginger, soy sauce, rice wine vinegar, lemon juice, sesame oil, chili paste, mayonnaise, and Tabasco. Mix well. Place dip in a serving bowl. Arrange with the skewers and have fun!

Duck

Throughout all the years that I have been experimenting with wild game, almost every time that I have mentioned wild duck, people have responded negatively. I almost cannot believe it. Restaurants all across the globe serve duck as one of their most beloved items. There are differences in domestic and wild ducks, and wild ducks win in flavor every time!

Wild ducks do have a more intense flavor than domestic ducks because they are usually older, leaner, denser, and smaller. Wild ducks eat from a variety of wild foods and fly long distances using muscle and building connective tissue. This adds to the flavor of the duck if prepared properly. Wild duck is easy to prepare, just a little different than domestic duck.

Dry aging is perfect for duck as well as for beef and venison. It helps to break down connective tissue and muscle fiber, making the duck much more tender. Remove breasts from the bone and place duck pieces in the refrigerator lightly covered for at least five days. Keep the duck from sitting in its own blood by placing the duck on a cooling rack on top of a cookie sheet and draining the blood from time to time. Remove duck and freeze in airtight bags or double wrap in freezer paper. Always remember to thaw in the refrigerator.

Cooking preparation is essential to the tenderness of the duck. Many people tend to overcook wild duck. Serving duck rare is by far my favorite application, but duck can also be braised in oil. Removing the fat from wild duck and replacing it with olive oil mixed with butter gives the duck an earthy flavor, and removes the gaminess that can be distasteful. Duck hunting is incredibly fun and enjoying wild duck at the dinner table… well, all the better.

Wild Duck Meatballs

Serves 4

  People who do not eat duck become duck lovers after eating these tasty meatballs. They are perfect for snacking or as a meal served over short-grained sticky rice or Chinese noodles.

HINT: Pancetta adds flavor and keeps the meatballs from drying out.

Ingredients

2 tablespoons of olive oil plus more for sautéing

1 medium yellow onion, minced

1 pear, peeled and finely chopped

2 teaspoons ginger, minced

2 cloves garlic, minced

2 pounds duck meat, cubed

½ pound pancetta

½ tablespoon kosher salt

1 teaspoon fresh thyme

1 teaspoon fresh rosemary, chopped

½ teaspoon Dijon mustard

½ teaspoon red pepper flakes

½ teaspoon cumin

½ teaspoon pepper

¼ cup parsley

½ cup white wine

1. Heat olive oil in a 10 to 12 inch sauté pan. Add onions, pears, ginger, and garlic until completely caramelized and liquid has evaporated. Chill for about an hour.

2. In a medium bowl, combine duck and pancetta along with the remaining ingredients. Chill for an hour.

3. Mix all ingredients together. Feed ingredients through a meat grinder with the medium die attachment.

4. Form 2-ounces balls from the meat mixture.

5. Heat 1 teaspoon olive oil in cast iron skillet until hot, but not smoking. Brown meatballs in batches. Cook until done all the way through, about 7 minutes.

6. Deglaze the pan with white wine. Season to taste and pour over meatballs.

7. Sprinkle parsley over the top of meatballs. Serve with rice, mashed potatoes, creamed spinach, pasta, or orzo. For snacking, serve with honey or your favorite barbeque sauce.

Duck Hoagie with Chipotle Sauce and Cucumber Carrot Slaw

Serves 4

The fancy word for this dish is Confit. It means to simply poach the meat in oil. Surprisingly, this dish is not at all greasy. This technique traps the juices in, reducing the possibility of tough or dry meat. Traditionally chefs only use the dark meat of the duck, but for this tasty sandwich, the breast meat works perfectly. It is super easy and extra flavorful.

• You can treat just about any protein in this manner.

• This succulent meat is also great on pizza.

• Poaching duck and vegetables in oil until cooked through and then storing the meat covered in its fat was a traditional way of preservation.

Ingredients

2 duck breasts

3 tablespoons kosher salt

1 teaspoon pepper

1 teaspoon brown sugar

1 teaspoon cinnamon

½ teaspoon cayenne pepper

4-5 sprigs fresh rosemary

3 garlic cloves

Olive oil, enough to cover duck breasts

Cucumber Carrot Slaw

Chipotle Dipping Sauce (p. 37)

4 Ciabatta Rolls

1. Preheat oven to 225 degrees.

2. In a medium-sized bowl mix salt, pepper, brown sugar, cinnamon, and cayenne pepper. Season both sides of the duck breast with mixture. Place rosemary sprigs and garlic cloves in the casserole dish. Cover the duck with olive oil. Cover the pan with foil and cook for about 4-6 hours until tender.

3. Remove duck from casserole and place in a cast iron skillet over high heat. Sear both sides of the duck. Remove duck from skillet and shred with a fork.

4. Slice ciabatta rolls in half and spread Chipotle Dipping Sauce on the bottoms of the rolls. Place slaw over the sauce and top with shredded duck and top bun. Serve with Sweet Potato Fries.

Cucumber Carrot Slaw

Ingredients

2 medium-sized cucumbers

2 carrots

2 cups apple cider vinegar

1 lemon, juiced

½ teaspoon salt

¼ teaspoon pepper

1. Peel cucumber and carrots with a vegetable peeler into long, thin strips and place in a medium sized bowl.

2. In a separate bowl mix vinegar, lemon juice, salt and pepper. Pour over vegetables and marinade in refrigerator for at least 2 hours.

Duck Hoagie

Wild Duck with Spinach and Honey

Serves 4

This dish is packed full of flavor with the balance of bitterness in the spinach and the sweetness of the duck marinated in the honey mixture. It is an easy yet elegant and tasty dish for company.

- Spinach is one of the world's most nutrient filled foods. It lowers blood pressure, prevents skin infections, and helps maintain the strength in our bones. My favorite benefit is its function as an anti-inflammatory. I would rather take my tasty spinach than a handful of medicine any day.

Ingredients

½ cup extra virgin olive oil plus extra for sautéing

2 tablespoons honey plus extra for drizzling

3 tablespoons red wine vinegar

1 tablespoon red pepper flakes

8 duck breasts (4 ducks), fat separated, rinsed, and patted dry

Kosher salt and freshly ground pepper

1 onion, thinly sliced

1 garlic clove, minced

Grated zest and juice of 1 lemon

6 cups of spinach

1. In a large baking dish, combine oil, honey, vinegar, and red pepper flakes. Add the duck and marinate overnight in the refrigerator or for 2 hours at room temperature.

2. In a 10 to 12 inch sauté pan, heat about 3 tablespoons of olive oil over high heat. Add onion and sauté for about 8 minutes. Add garlic, zest and juice of lemon, and spinach and cook until wilted, 2 to 3 minutes. Season with salt and pepper.

3. Meanwhile heat oil in cast iron skillet. Remove duck from marinade. Salt and pepper generously. When skillet is hot but not smoky, place duck in skillet for about 5 minutes. Turn for another 4 minutes. Remove from pan and let rest for about 5 minutes.

4. Divide spinach among 4 plates. Cut duck on the bias and arrange over the spinach. Drizzle with about 2 tablespoons of honey. Serve immediately.

Quail

Quail is a small bird that is native to North America. Quail are a species of the edge. As large farms started overtaking the small family-owned farms, there became less desirable habitat for the quail. Quail enjoy open woods, fields, and native grasses. Many of the corporate farms have miles of open expanses. Quail, being ground-dwellers, are also subject to their natural predators: cats, skunks, fox, raccoons, owls, snakes, dogs, and fire ants. The life span of quail is less than one year and the chicks have a 30% mortality rate. There are many organizations dedicated to preserving wild quail such as Quail Unlimited.

If you do not have access to hunt wild quail, there are many high-end supermarkets that carry them in the freezer section. Quail are incredibly flavorful and are worthy to become one of your staple foods. They are small and therefore cook quickly, making meals with quail great for entertaining or just a quick easy meal for your family.

I am hoping that quail will begin to repopulate the United States quickly. Many hunters are inadvertently enhancing quail habitat by managing their land for deer and turkey. We have personally seen an increase of quail on our managed farm in the past five years and are continuing to create better habitat for the quail.

HOW TO:
DEBONE A QUAIL

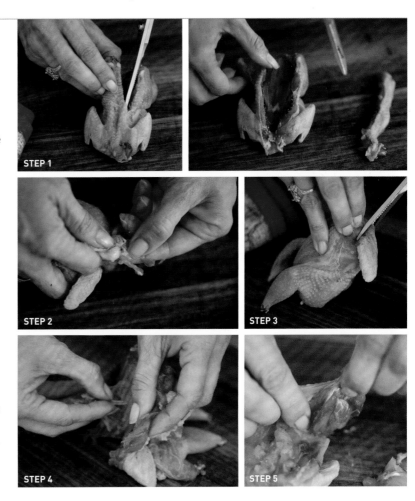

Step 1

With the bird facing up, cut down each side of the backbone with kitchen scissors.

Step 2

Remove the wishbone by reaching into the neck cavity, massaging around the wishbone and pulling it out.

Step 3

With kitchen scissors, cut the wing joint (shoulder) to disconnect from ribcage.

Step 4

Remove ribcage by massaging the meat from the ribs. Be careful near the sternum because there is very little meat and it is only held together with skin. If recipe calls for a semi-deboned quail, this would be your last step.

Step 5   Massage meat away from leg bones as in step 4. Wings are left for presentation.

Stuffed Quail with Figs and Prosciutto

Serves 4

The creaminess of the grits and beans pairs beautifully with the sweet figs, salty prosciutto, and rosemary-infused quail. This meal is a true Southern delight that you will desire time and again.

Ingredients

4 boneless quail

16 figs, divided

¼ pound prosciutto, chopped

4 sprigs rosemary, 4 inches long

Kosher salt

Freshly ground pepper

Olive oil for browning and grilling

2 cups white beans, cooked and seasoned

Cheesy grits (p. 83)

1. Preheat oven to 375 degrees.

2. Begin preparing grits and warming beans.

3. Chop 12 figs and place in a bowl with chopped prosciutto. Combine and set aside.

4. Season each quail with salt and pepper. Lay quail skin side down on a plate or cutting board. Place fig and prosciutto stuffing in the center of the quail and wrap quail around the stuffing and secure with a rosemary sprig.

5. Heat olive oil in a cast iron skillet over high heat until almost smoking. Place quail breasts side down for about three minutes or until brown. Turn over and cook another 3 minutes.

6. Meanwhile heat grill over high heat. Slice remaining figs lengthwise and place flesh side down on grill for about 2 minutes. Remove from grill and set aside.

7. Place skillet into oven and cook quail for 3 to 5 minutes. Remove quail from oven.

8. Ladle about ½ cup of grits into four plates. Place the quail on the grits and serve with beans and grilled figs.

Pan Fried Quail

Serves 4

If you want a quick meal full of flavor, this is the meal for you. It takes only minutes to caramelize the spicy sweet quail and have it over salad greens, sweet potatoes, or grits and satisfy your most ravenous cravings.

Ingredients

8 quail, deboned

¼ cup olive oil for browning

2 tablespoons cumin

1 tablespoon freshly ground pepper

½ teaspoon red pepper flakes

½ teaspoon cayenne pepper

2 tablespoons honey

½ teaspoon salt

1. In a medium-sized bowl, mix cumin, pepper, red pepper flakes, cayenne, honey, and salt. Place quail in marinade for about 5 minutes.

2. Drizzle olive oil into a super hot skillet. When olive oil is shimmering, place quail in skillet for 3 minutes. Turn over and cook the other side for about 2 minutes. Remove the quail from the skillet and serve with Mashed Sweet Potatoes (p. 35).

Rustic Quail Pizza

Yields 2 Pizzas

    In my opinion this pizza can't be beat! My daughter started making this recipe about a year ago and weekly I hear her brothers and sisters beg, "Please make your pizza!" We often use quail, venison or whatever left-over meat we have as a topping. It's easy to make and its bold flavors bring comforting satisfaction.

• Make a double batch of dough and freeze one of the batches for those extra busy days.

• If you don't have all of these ingredients, be creative and use whatever you have on hand. I prefer quail, but any wild game is great as well as leaving it as a veggie pizza.

• You can replace tomatillos with green tomatoes.

Ingredients

8 cups self-rising flour, extra for dusting
1 tablespoon kosher salt
1 tablespoon active dry yeast
2 ¾ cups warm water

Topping Ingredients

1 pint crushed tomatoes
4 cloves garlic, minced
Juice of one lime
1 tablespoon of thyme
½ cup of olive oil, for browning and
    sautéing
1 medium eggplant, skin removed and
    thinly sliced
4 tomatillos, husked and thinly sliced
1 pound mushrooms
1 cup cherry tomatoes, halved
1 pound prosciutto, sliced
1 pound provolone, sliced
Meat of 4 Pain Fried Quail
½ cup basil, chopped
Kosher salt to taste
2 ½ cups parmesan cheese

1. Preheat oven to 400 degrees.

2. In a medium-sized bowl, mix flour and salt. Sprinkle yeast over flour and slowly begin to incorporate warm water into the flour with clean hands or a wooden spoon. Using all of the water may not be necessary. Place dough in a non-humid location and let rest for 30 minutes.

3. Meanwhile, place crushed tomatoes, garlic, lime juice and thyme in a medium-sized bowl and puree with a stick blender. If you do not have a stick blender place all ingredients in a food processor and puree.

4. Heat 2 tablespoons of olive oil in a large sauté pan. When oil is shimmering add vegetables in batches until vegetables are soft.

5. Sprinkle flour onto work surface and place dough onto the floured surface. Split dough into two equal parts with a knife or a dough scraper. Starting from the center, roll out one of the dough balls into a ⅛ inch thick rectangle. If dough is too sticky, sprinkle a little flour on dough and continue to roll. Place dough on a cookie sheet. Repeat with other dough ball.

6. Divide toppings between the two pizzas by first adding the sauce, leaving an inch around the sides then add vegetable toppings. Continue layering each pizza with provolone, prosciutto, and meat from the Pan Fried Quail. Lightly sprinkle entire pizza with salt, including the edges. Sprinkle basil and parmesan cheese evenly over pizzas.

7. Bake pizzas for 35 minutes or until golden brown and cheese is bubbly. Serve immediately.

Rustic Quail Pizza

Small Game

Hunting small game is one of my boys' favorite pastimes. Being extremely quick and alert creatures, it takes more skill than one might think to harvest them. The boys were in awe when my oldest girl proclaimed that she was going squirrel hunting in the back yard, and within minutes she was cleaning her harvest and preparing to cook it! I especially like the skills that hunting small game teaches. It teaches self restraint, stalking skills, being quiet and observant, teamwork, and incredible marksmanship!

Small game does not get the culinary recognition that it deserves. Many dishes dating back centuries used squirrel and rabbit. Our ancestors had no choice but to kill their own meat and prepare it for meals. Full of woodsy earthy flavor, dishes such as Brunswick Stew remains a favorite today. Many high-end restaurants serve squirrel and rabbit as a delicacy and at very high prices. Chefs know that the rich flavor of this game is exceptional and worth every penny.

You will find that these critters are quite easy to prepare. They are perfect for stews and braises, therefore a slow cooker and pressure cooker are excellent tools for their preparation. Frying is also a fantastic option after soaking in a marinade or buttermilk bath overnight. If dressed quickly from the field, hastily chilled, and thoroughly cooked, you will have the meal of your life.

Classic Brunswick Stew

Serves 6 to 8

As a diversion from school, the boys will hunt squirrel between subjects. At the beginning of squirrel season the kids decide on a prize for the most squirrels harvested. They are very intense and professional about the competition. They even have a rules manual and a chart graphically designed on the computer!

Ingredients

- 3-4 squirrels (about 12 oz.) dressed and cut into ½ inch cubes
- 1 cup flour
- 2 tablespoons kosher salt, divided
- 1 teaspoon freshly ground pepper, divided
- ½ cup olive oil
- 1 cup celery, diced

- 1 cup onion, diced
- 1 cup bell pepper, diced
- 1 cup carrots, diced
- 4 garlic cloves, minced
- 1 cup corn
- 1 pint homemade canned tomatoes or 1 14 oz. can of tomatoes
- ½ cup turnips, diced

- 1 cup Yukon gold potatoes, diced
- 2 teaspoons rosemary
- 1 teaspoon thyme
- 2 bay leaves
- 1½ cups dry white wine
- 1 cup okra cut into ½-inch pieces
- 3 cups chicken stock
- Lemon juice

1. In a large bowl, mix flour, 1 tablespoon salt, and ½ teaspoon pepper. Place squirrel in bowl with flour mixture and coat thoroughly.

2. In a large Dutch oven, heat olive oil until almost smoking. Sauté squirrel in batches. Remove squirrel and set aside.

3. Add celery, onions, bell pepper, carrots and garlic to the pot. Add more olive oil for sautéing if needed. Cook until vegetables are translucent over medium heat. Add remaining tablespoon of salt and ½ teaspoon pepper.

4. Add corn, tomatoes, turnips, Yukon gold potatoes, rosemary, thyme, bay leaves, wine, okra, chicken stock and squirrel meat to the pot. Bring mixture to a boil then lower to simmer for about 35 minutes. Add extra water if necessary. Squeeze the juice of one lemon over stew. Serve with cornbread.

Classic Brunswick Stew

Fried Rabbit and Sage Buttermilk Waffles

Fried Rabbit and Sage Buttermilk Waffles

Serves 4

Waffles and fried chicken have been a tradition in my household as long as I can remember. Every one of my favorite foods is contained in this one mouthwatering dish!

Ingredients

1 rabbit, quartered and deboned

1 cup buttermilk

2 cups all-purpose flour

1 ½ tablespoons paprika

1 teaspoon kosher salt

½ teaspoon freshly ground pepper

Tabasco

3 cups of vegetable oil for frying

Sage Buttermilk Waffles

Honey Butter Sauce (p. 75)

Maple syrup for serving

1. Debone rabbit and soak in buttermilk overnight in a baking dish or zip-top bag.

2. Combine flour, paprika, salt and pepper in a shallow dish.

3. Place a wire rack on a baking sheet and set aside.

4. Remove rabbit and discard buttermilk. Season rabbit with a few shakes of Tabasco. Dredge rabbit in flour mixture.

5. Pour oil in skillet to a depth of about ¾ inch. Oil should reach 350 degrees. Fry the rabbit in batches about 5 minutes on one side, then turn and fry for 3 to 4 minutes on the other side. Move the rabbit to the wire rack on the cookie sheet and let rest. To keep warm while making the waffles place in a 200-degree oven. Serve with Sage Waffles, Honey Butter Sauce, and Maple syrup.

Sage Buttermilk Waffles

Ingredients

1¾ cups flour

3 tablespoons sugar

3 tablespoons yellow cornmeal

½ teaspoon baking soda

½ teaspoon salt

2 cups buttermilk

1 tablespoon sage

2 tablespoons Dijon mustard

2 eggs

8 tablespoons butter, melted

1. In a medium-sized bowl, combine flour, sugar, cornmeal, baking soda, and salt.

2. In another medium-sized bowl, whisk buttermilk, sage, mustard, and eggs.

3. Add wet ingredients into the dry ingredients and whisk melted butter into mixture.

4. Heat an oiled waffle iron and pour batter onto the griddle. Cook until crisped and golden brown. You will know it is ready when steam stops releasing from your waffle iron. Transfer the waffles to a serving plate and repeat with remaining batter. To keep waffles warm, place them in a 200 degree oven until ready to use.

Seafood and Fish

Our family enjoys every kind of fishing, but especially deep sea fishing. We try to go on a deep sea fishing trip at least once yearly, with grandparents and friends. It is such fun to see the catch when they return to shore. Everyone usually has enough healthy fish to last until the next opportunity to go again.

We have many lakes and creeks around our community to catch bass, bream, catfish, and crappie. We love to canoe down the creek on our land and fly fish for red-eye bass and bream. We also like to canoe to the Coosa River and spend the day catching white bass. The kids also love a diversion from studying by going fishing with my dad to his favorite fishing hole "where the water is crystal clear".

Doctors and nutritionists around the world recommend that we eat a diet containing at least two servings of fish a week. For years, we have known that people following this recommendation are less susceptible to heart disease, diabetes, and cancer. In addition to its health benefits, fish is also quick and easy to prepare. You can have a delicious, healthy, gourmet meal on the table within 20 minutes.

Naturally caught fish eat plankton, crustaceans, insects, and other fish found in the water, while farm-raised fish feast on corn and grains that are often filled with additives to make them grow faster. As a result, farm-raised fish are often far less healthy than fish that live in the wild.

Herb Pecan Crusted Trout

Serves 4

This dish is great for easy entertaining. The flavor of the trout is so mild that even the pickiest eaters will love it.

Ingredients

¾ cups pecans, finely chopped

2 tablespoons rosemary, finely chopped

¼ cup fresh parsley, finely chopped and divided

½ teaspoon salt

½ teaspoon pepper

1½ tablespoons Dijon mustard

4 6-ounce trout fillets, skinned

Olive oil, for browning

2 tablespoons butter, plus more for browning

1 lemon, juiced

¼ cup white wine

3 tablespoons capers

2 cups spinach

2 cups arugula

1. On a plate, combine pecans, rosemary, half the parsley, salt and pepper.

2. Lightly brush one side of fillet with Dijon mustard and press fillet into the pecan mixture to adhere. Set aside and proceed with remaining fillets.

3. Heat about 1 tablespoon each of olive oil and butter over medium-high heat. When oil is sizzling hot, place fillets pecan-batter side down in pan and cook for about 3 minutes. Do not crowd the pan; you might have to cook in batches. Flip fillets and cook for about 2 more minutes, or until flaky and golden. Remove fillets to platter and tent with foil. Repeat with remaining fillets.

4. Once all fillets are cooked, add the butter, lemon juice, and wine to deglaze the pan. The brown bits from the fish are truly golden nuggets to be cherished! Add capers and bring to a boil. Turn off heat and stir in rest of parsley.

5. Prepare plates with spinach and arugula and top each one with a fillet. Divide wine sauce evenly among the plates and serve immediately.

Fish Tacos

Serves 4-6

Fish tacos are one of our family's favorite summer time staples. After a day of fishing, we come home, pick fresh herbs and sit out on the porch eating this scrumptious treat making great memories.

• You can substitute any white flaky fish for this recipe.

Ingredients

2 cups Vidalia onions, chopped

½ cup fresh cilantro

2 cloves garlic, minced

2 teaspoons oregano

½ teaspoon salt

⅓ cup olive oil

¼ cup lime juice, plus wedges of lime for garnish

4 scamp fillets

12 small flour tortillas

Lime mayonnaise

3 avocados, sliced

Pica de Gallo (p. 101)

1. In a medium bowl, mix onions, cilantro, garlic, oregano, salt, oil, and lime juice. Pour half the mixture into a 9- ×11-inch casserole. Place fish fillets on top of mixture. Pour the remaining marinade over fish. Cover and chill for 1 hour.

2. Heat griddle on grill to almost smoking. Place fillets on hot grill for 2–3 minutes. Turn and cook for another 2–3 minutes or until fish is opaque. Remove from heat and set aside.

3. Grill tortillas for about 10 seconds per side.

4. Coarsely chop fish and place on tortilla. Drizzle lime mayonnaise on top of fish and place avocado and Pico de Gallo on top. Serve with lemon or lime wedges.

Lime Mayonnaise

HINT: If you need a shortcut use mayonnaise and mix with lime juice.

• All ingredients must be at room temperature.

Ingredients

1 egg

2 egg yolks

2 tablespoons lime juice

1 teaspoon Dijon mustard

½ teaspoon salt

Dash of Tabasco sauce

2 cups olive oil

1. In a food processor, add egg, egg yolks, lime juice, mustard, salt, and Tabasco sauce.

2. Start food processor and run continually while very slowly adding drops off oil, waiting 10 seconds between each drop. Continue with the drops for about ¼ cup of oil.

3. When mayonnaise has definitely thickened, add oil in a stream. You may not need all the oil at this time, therefore, check after each ½ cup is added for thickness and taste. If the consistency is very thick, add a drop of lime to thin it or if too thin add more oil.

4. Place mayonnaise in a bowl and serve or keep covered in refrigerator for 1 week.

Greek Snapper

Serves 6

This dish is incredibly easy to make, but is packed full of flavor. You could substitute any white flaky fish for the snapper and make the dish a weekly staple.

Ingredients

2 -3 tablespoons olive oil

2 pounds fresh snapper (about 2 large fillets)

½ teaspoon salt

¼ teaspoon pepper

½ Vidalia onion, chopped

½ cup Kalamata olives

3 tablespoons capers

1 tablespoon garlic, minced

1 tablespoon fresh rosemary, chopped

1 pint (1 can) canned tomatoes

½ cup dry white wine

1. Preheat oven to 200 degrees.

2. Drizzle about 2 tablespoons of olive oil in a large sauté pan over medium-high heat. Salt and pepper fillets and place in pan when oil is shimmering. Cook for 5 minutes and then turn fillets over and cook for another 3-5 minutes or until fish flakes easily. Place gently onto a cookie sheet and place into oven with door cracked to keep warm.

3. Add remaining olive oil to pan. Sauté onions, olives, capers, garlic, and rosemary for about 5 minutes. Add tomatoes and wine to the medley and reduce for 5- 10 more minutes.

4. Remove snapper from oven, place on platter, and pour olive mixture over the fish. Serve with a side salad and a crusty bread.

Crappie With White Bean and Basil

Serves 4 to 6

Creamy beans and Crappie is the ultimate fish comfort food. The creaminess of the beans with the flakiness of the fish and a few shakes of Tabasco is to me the perfect fish dish. While eating this mild, white, flaky fish, I am reminded that summer is just around the corner.

• If you are in a hurry, use canned cannellini or navy beans. Rinse the beans and add about ¼ cup water to the bean mixture in the recipe.

Ingredients

¾ cup white beans

6 crappie fillets

Kosher salt

Freshly ground black pepper

Olive oil for sautéing

1 teaspoon fresh basil, plus extra for garnish; chopped

1 teaspoon fresh parsley, plus extra for garnish; chopped

½ lemon, juiced

1. Place white beans in a medium pot with water covering beans 2 inches. Bring water to boil, then lower heat to a simmer for about 45 minutes.

2. Meanwhile, season crappie fillets liberally with salt and pepper.

3. Drizzle olive oil into a heated sauté pan. When oil is shimmering, place crappie in pan and cook for 3 minutes. Lower heat to medium. Turn over fillet and cook for another 2–3 minutes. Remove from heat and repeat with remaining fillets.

4. Add basil, parsley, and lemon juice to the beans and bring back to boil, and then lower to simmer.

5. Season beans with salt and divide among 6 shallow bowls. Top the beans with the crappie fillet. Garnish with remaining chopped basil and parsley, and a drizzle of olive oil.

Best Ever Clam Bake

Serves 8

We recently celebrated two birthdays on the same day and no, they are not twins. My oldest son and my oldest daughter are five years apart. On every birthday each child gets to choose his or her favorite meal and dessert. At least four out of seven birthdays we will have our famous clambake. The seafood is incredibly beautiful and it looks as if it took hours to prepare, but in reality it only takes about 30 minutes to make. Not only is this dish tasty and beautiful, the clean up time is minimal as well! How great is that?

HINT: Splitting the lobster lengthwise down the middle of the tail's underside keeps the tail from curling during cooking.

Ingredients

½ cup olive oil

2 large onions, chopped

6 cloves garlic

2 pounds red potatoes

2 pounds kielbasa, sliced 1-inch thick diagonally

1 tablespoon salt

½ tablespoon freshly ground pepper

6 sprigs thyme

3 cups good white wine

1 cup fish stock

6 ears of corn, husked and snapped in half

3 dozen little neck clams, scrubbed

1 lobster tail, split lengthwise down the flesh

1 ½ pounds large shrimp, deveined and in the shell

2 pounds mussels, de-bearded and cleaned

3 tablespoons butter

1. In a 20-quart pot, sauté onions in olive oil for 15 minutes or until onions start to brown. Put garlic into pot and cook for 2 more minutes.

2. Place potatoes, kielbasa, salt, pepper, and thyme on top of the onions and pour in the white wine and fish stock. Cover with a lid and cook medium high heat for 20 minutes.

3. Place corn, clams, and lobster into pot for 5 minutes. Cover the pot tightly.

4. Add the shrimp and mussels to the pot for 5 minutes. Test the potatoes for tenderness. The lobster and shrimp should be opaque and the clams and mussels should be opened. If not, cook a few more minutes.

5. With a large slotted spoon, remove the vegetables and seafood to a large bowl.

6. Add 3 tablespoons of butter to the broth and bring to a boil. Season to taste. Serve over the clambake. Serve with crusty bread.

Index

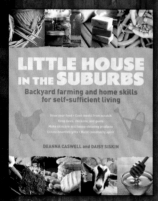